Douglas Harding has produced a long list of books on the good life over the past sixty years (which have been published in Chinese and Japanese as well as the main European languages). He is still, in partnership with his wife Catherine, at the age of 93, busy touring the world conducting workshops for sharing his unique vision of the treasure that lies concealed at the heart of the great traditional faiths. Participants in these workshops have varied from more than 2000 to less than 20 at a time. But common to them all is the fact that it is not what he says that persuades people and can drastically transform their lives, but the unique tests or experiments that he has devised for arriving at conscious union with our Source - alias the Beatific Vision - and for putting that happy realisation into daily practice. He lives near Ipswich in Suffolk.

Further information about the work of D.E. Harding, contact:
The Sholland Trust
87B Cazenove Road
London
NW16 6BB
Email: headexchange@gn.apc.org
Website: www.headless.org

To Be
and not
To Be

that is the answer

UNIQUE EXPERIMENTS FOR TAPPING
OUR INFINITE RESOURCES

D E HARDING

Watkins Publishing
London

This edition published in the UK in 2002 by
Watkins Publishing, 20 Bloomsbury Street,
London, WC1B 3QA

© Douglas Harding 2002

Douglas Harding has asserted his right under the Copyright,
Designs and Patents Act, 1988, to be identified as author of
this work.

Cover design by Echelon Design, Wimborne
Cover photograph © PhotoDisk
Designed and typeset by Echelon Design, Wimborne
Printed and bound in Great Britain by NFF Production

British Library Cataloguing in Publication data available

Library of Congress Cataloging in Publication data available

ISBN 1 84293 044 3

www.watkinspublishing.com

Contents

OBLIGATORY
INTRODUCTION

Nearly every chapter in this book started life as a magazine article complete in itself. The result is that you can read the chapters in any order you fancy. But if this is the first book of mine that you are reading, and you haven't been to any of my workshops, I think it would be a good thing to take them in the order given.

The book as a whole has three essential components. In order of increasing importance they are: the words and the case they make, the maps and diagrams, and the exercises or experiments. The first for reading, the second for giving shape and order to what you read about, the third for doing, for actively turning overvalued and wishy-washy concepts into down-to-earth percepts. (Just to read about the exercises without doing them would be to miss their point and reduce the book to gobbledegook.)

There are four basic experiments, and a growing number of subsidiary ones (some twenty, to date). They all serve the same purpose, which is to take us Home to the Place we never really left. To where we actually *see* that we Are because we Are Not, are Everything because we are Nothing Whatever.

Each chapter, being self-contained, deploys whatever experiments and diagrams it needs in order to make its point. This is why, when you come to other chapters, you will find that you are asked to repeat experiments that you have already done. This is all to the good: the experiments are also exercises for repeating. They can't be carried out too often or in too many contexts. In fact they are for deliberately building into our everyday life till they are no longer set up, but come into practice quite naturally, without effort or any apparatus, as occasion demands. For example, the Tunnel Experiment (which – among other startling revelations – shows me that I've never been face-to-face with anybody in my life) has to be done till it does itself whenever I happen to see a face.

Another reason for repeating the experiments is that we don't repeat them! Every time is a first time. They are for getting used to *doing*, never for getting used to. Here's an instance. In workshops conducted round the world over the last thirty-five years, I must have carried out the Tunnel Experiment upwards of 2,000 times with ten times that number of people. And the last time (which was five days ago) I found it more surprising and revealing than ever. You could say that our experiments take on the timelessness of their Subject-Matter, of the Being-NonBeing that is only Here and only Now.

So a warm welcome from me, Douglas Harding, and from Catherine my wife and co-worker, to what some of our friends call our God Lab.

How can I begin to list, much less to thank adequately, the many friends who have helped and taught and encouraged me in this much-needed laboratory work? My very special gratitude goes to Catherine, to whom I dedicate this book.

1

To Be And Not To Be

I hesitate to say exactly what Hamlet means (or what Shakespeare meant Hamlet to mean) by his famous soliloquy 'To be or not to be - that is the question'. Shakespearean scholars will tell you. What it means to me is as follows.

I have a choice, at times an agonising choice between two evils. On the one hand is life - life which is sweet and sour, pleasurable and very painful, sometimes easy but usually difficult and sometimes excruciatingly difficult. On the other hand is death, which presents itself as relief from pain - at the cost of annihilation and endless oblivion, and it's a terrifying prospect. Put it like this: to exist is nasty, while to cease to exist is at least as nasty, but in a different way. So here's the dilemma I'm faced with: shall I go on living the life I'm living, or shall I opt out of it, either by drugging myself into a stupor (and there are countless approved and disapproved opiates to choose from) or by killing myself outright? In brief, to be or not to be - that is the question that's tearing my life apart. Of all questions this is the one that demands an answer.

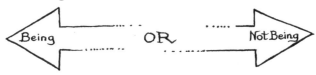

Here's mine in a nutshell. The life I'm living consists of two contrasting elements. (1) *There* are all manner of ever-changing things – sticks and stones and somebody's bones, arms and a trunk and legs, people and animals and plants, planets and stars and galaxies, goodness and truth and beauty along with their opposites, sensations and emotions and thoughts of all kinds, and so on and on and on. (2) *Here* is the unchanging No-thing that's in receipt of all those things, the arena they perform in, the conscious Emptiness that makes way for them, that disappears in their favour. Here I'm the absence they are present in and presented to. And it's because these two elements of which I'm composed are totally contrasted that they dovetail so neatly, coming together in seamless unity.

Being and Not-being are the two faces of the same coin of pure gold. It is because, like Hamlet, we are split down the middle, that the currency of our life is debased and we are miserably poor. But when at last we bring the two faces of the coin together, and we are no longer cases of Being *or* Not-being but of Being *and* Not-being, we find ourselves rich beyond compare and all our life is transformed.

How does this new life work out in practice?

My experience, whatever its kind, is a two-way, is-isn't affair. What I call "my attention" takes the form of this double arrow pointing out to the Object that is and simultaneously in to the Subject that isn't. For instance the conventional face-to-face set-up is replaced by

Living this way consciously, instead of unconsciously as hitherto, makes a lot of difference. This bipolar vision, exercised in all the changing circumstances of life, is truly practical. For example, you and I, insofar as we no longer see ourselves as face to face, cease confronting and opposing one another. I'm not denying that much practice of the vision is needed for it to become steady and habitual. But I can assure you that no practice is wasted, and that it may not take you that long to get rid of morbid self-consciousness, if it happens to plague you as it did me. And the reason why it works so well, and in so many different ways, is simple. It works because it goes back to nature, to our true Nature. This is the way we are built. Here, form is void, our Nature is no-Nature, I am not-I, to be is not to be, he who loses his life shall save it, One becomes Nought. Every being – and notably Being Itself – owes its being to its replacement by other beings. The power and the glory behind the world is love – where love, as in tennis, is zero.

The following chapters explore, from various starting points, this infinitely creative and clearly visible (but wildly paradoxical and mysterious) Union of Being and Non-being. I hope they will help to show that all you could possibly desire is wrapped up in the realisation and enjoyment of that Union.

Meantime let's take encouragement from that great Spanish poet and seer, St. John of the Cross: "To have all things I must have nothing, to know all things I must know nothing, to be all things I must be nothing." And let's take warning from that great English poet and seer, William Blake: "Lest the Last Judgement come and find me unannihilate, and I be seized and given into the hands of my own selfhood."

2

TREASURE TROVE

If, in all seriousness, I were to tell you that hidden in your house was a priceless six-sided diamond, exactly where to find it, and precisely what each lovely facet of the diamond looked like, what would you do? Would you yawn, and change the subject as quickly as possible? No! Would you believe me, and do nothing about it? No! Would you disbelieve me, and leave it at that? No! Would you feel so uncomfortable and so threatened that you avoided that spot from now on? Emphatically No! On the contrary, you would rush there headlong to see whether I was speaking the truth.

Well, I withdraw the IF. What I'm telling you is gospel truth. This most valuable of treasures is absolutely real and absolutely yours. Here, at your very Centre and Home-base, in the Place that's closer to you than your breathing, in the Place you are looking out of, shines this precious jewel. Don't believe me or disbelieve me. Just do yourself the favour of looking carefully to see what's your side of what you see, taking it in. I assure you it is none other than that Jewel, possessed of which you have all your heart could desire.

At this stage, probably, it all sounds far too good to be true, and you tell me that what you are looking out of couldn't be less jewel-like. Our trouble is that while we are pretty good at seeing what we are looking AT (such as the people and cars in the street that have to be avoided – or else …) we are very bad at looking in the other direction, very bad indeed at seeing what we are looking OUT OF. Much worse than that, we hallucinate wildly here, superimposing on the beautiful and amazing and beneficent Facts ugly and boring and desperately miserable fictions. Well, our business in the following chapters is to correct this tragic mistake, and to find out whether, beyond all possibility of doubt, the Facts are (to put it mildly) favourable. As favourable as the fictions that hide them are unfavourable. Favourable, and brilliantly on show.

I'm confident that, with the help of our experiments, you will find that you don't *possess* this six-sided Treasure, but that you *are* it. That this is your true Identity. What can you lose, what do you stand to gain, by looking in at what's brilliantly on display here, and giving it a trial. And going on to discover just how many of your problems arise from your pretending to be, in all important respects, the poverty-stricken opposite of the radiant Marvel that you now clearly see you are.

Meanwhile, here is the Scottish clergyman and novelist George Macdonald: "At length the glory of our existence flashes upon us, we face full to the Sun that enlightens what it sent forth, and know ourselves alive with an infinite life." I believe the chances are that, sooner than you think, you'll be saying that he got it right.

3

WHERE AM I?

If you cease overlooking
the Nothing at your Centre
it will explode into Everything
which includes and so saves you.
If you go on overlooking it
it will go on as the Nothing
which excludes and destroys you.

This chapter gives a condensed account of a workshop run by my wife Catherine and myself, Douglas Harding. We work as a duo, a team, but don't plan in advance who shall do what. In fact we have no fixed agenda and are ready for surprises.

As far as possible I record pictorially on a white-board the conclusions we come to and the discoveries we make in the course of the workshop. The results figure as the illustrations in this chapter.

We start with a quotation from Eric Berne, the author of *Games People Play* and the founder of Transactional Analysis. "We are all born princes and princesses, but the business of society is to turn us into frogs." Well, we add, the business of this workshop is to turn us back into princes and princesses.

But first we have to take an uncompromisingly honest look at our present froggy-human condition. We don't get to be princely by sweeping under the carpet all evidence of the desperate trouble we are in. On the contrary, we make it much worse. And certainly we will never discover, let alone take, the medicine that does exist for our disease, till we realise just how serious and many-levelled that disease is. It's for these reasons that we start off this workshop by being very miserable. It's a small price to pay for ending on the happiest of notes. Yes, we promise to come up with the cure for our condition, in due course.

Let's first look at the handicaps that go with being human, that belong to man's own level in the scheme of things.

Here he is, this fellow who's in trouble.

We have only to look at him to see how solitary, how lonely that little fellow is, how done up in a separate, tightly-wrapped parcel, distinct from and distant from all the other human parcels. I'm shut up with my pain, which is as unshareable as my experience of fried bacon and eggs – of their taste and texture and smell and colour and sound. Strangers confronting one another, opposed face-to-face and frequently at loggerheads – when Tom wins Dick and Harry lose – we must expect unending head-on collisions.

And much fear. The great fear, of course, is the fear of death, from which (we are told) all lesser fears spring. How very brief life is! My 92 years have gone in a flash. But we suppress by every means the fact that we are all sitting in death-row awaiting execution, which may be at any moment. And, so far from getting rid of the fear of *our own* death by refusing to think about it or speak about it, we only pile on the agony. (Other people's deaths, of course, are another matter.)

Again, how much of our experience *hurts* in some degree! He is indeed fortunate the sum of whose pleasures outweighs the sum of his pains. Let's be as honest as the Buddha about life's unsatisfactoriness. Until we admit it we are unlikely to seek – much less discover and take up residence in – the Place that's perfectly satisfactory and satisfying.

16

What about poverty, about the many things – material, psychological, spiritual – that we want but can't get? And how long is it before the things we do get get us, possess us? O for the goods that stay good, for the true riches that really enrich their owners!

We could go on to moan about the embarrassing messiness of man as an unremitting wellspring of tons and tons of filth, which pathetic euphemisms like *ladies and gents* and *toilet* and *comfort station* or *powder room* do their best to hush up. Or moan about the humbling similarity of his lovemaking to that of the flies on the bedroom windowpane. But we think we have made the point that the human lot is not one that humans are happy about, and that if there's a remedy (and we promise you there is) we should go for it hell for leather.

As if this many-sided tale of woe at our human level weren't enough, we are in terrible trouble at what you might call our supra-human levels.

Like Catherine and me, you are just one of 6,000,000,000 humans circumambulating this planet, which is just one of billions of planets and planetoids circumambulating this Sun, which is just one of billions of stars circumambulating this galaxy, which is just one of billions of galaxies. And goodness knows how many myriads of stars in all these galaxies have developed into solar systems with planets inhabited by creatures comparable to but vastly different from ourselves. We ask you: could you be more lost, more insignificant than you are in these immensities of space and time and stuff? Could our life, with all its agonies and ecstasies be more meaningless than it is in such a setting? A sand-grain in the Sahara is more meaningful and important in and to the Sahara than we are in such a Universe!

Is turning a blind eye to our status in the Cosmos the price of sanity for us humans? Is dishonesty here the best policy? We say No! Here's trouble in plenty: let's not add deliberate narrow-mindedness and self-deception to the trouble. But is a remedy for the dreadful disease of meaninglessness *conceivable* in such a Cosmos? The chances of our finding and tasting it before the conclusion of this workshop seem remote. But let's see.

Meanwhile, there's worse to come. We have still to address the most insidious and immediately threatening of our troubles. At the human level the pain, the loneliness, the warfare, the death sentence; at suprahuman levels the lostness and the meaninglessness; at infrahuman levels the conditioning, the victimisation, the slavery.

"What are little girls made of?" we used to ask. We replied: "sugar and spice and all things nice", but nowa-days our story is less reassuring. We girls and boys are made of millions and millions of tiny animals of many species, not all of whom are consistently dedicated to our best interests. And each in turn is made of non-living things called molecules that are laws unto themselves. And the same can be said of the atoms they consist of, which are mostly empty space. And so on down to our ultimate ingredients, whatever they are. Mathematising physicists find their way around these mysterious regions, or get lost in them. We get lost.

And we have plenty to worry about at all five infrahuman levels: cells, molecules, atoms, particles and quarks. Regardless of my wants and wishes, this immense interior population of mine rules me with a rod of iron, a cat-o'-five-tails. I didn't consent to being a man instead of a woman, to my liability to minor strokes, to being fat rather than thin, to being irritable rather than even-tempered, to suffering the early stages of the disease (whatever it is) that I'm shortly going to die of. In countless respects I'm the unwilling victim of all manner of secretive and petty but powerful dictators, from my genes and chromosomes all the way down to and beyond the quark.

We humans go on and on about freedom. Liberty takes precedence over fraternity and equality according to Catherine, who's French. But what price freedom now, under the searchlight of the biological and physical sciences? Can you think of a more insidious and unrelenting and many-sided bondage than the interior bondage that we humans suffer? Can we *begin* to imagine a Spartacan uprising against such masters?

So where have we got to, in our tale of human woe?

We are in treble trouble. The pain of our human level, the meaninglessness of our suprahuman levels, and the slavery of our infrahuman levels.

Why have we found it necessary to be so negative about the human condition? We answer this question by asking another question. Why haven't we done what most of us do most of the time – which is sweep all that unpleasantness under the carpet, suppress it, know it in abstract and general terms when applied to others, while refusing to know it in concrete and particular terms when applied to ourselves? Why haven't we joined the ranks of those countless educated and intelligent folk who with all their might insist that they are "only human after all"? In other words, why don't we go on pretending that we are just frogs who by no means spill over into the swamp underfoot or the dark sky overhead? Just frogs.

Well, considering how menacing our real situation turns out to be, it is perhaps no wonder that we opt for a dream-life with frequent nightmares. And no wonder that, as a result, our lives should be unrealistic and unpractical in countless ways, as well as centuries behind the scientific times. And certainly no wonder that we should miss out on the medicine for the menace.

Catherine interrupts here. Enough is Enough. The time has come for us to seek the medicine. For a start, let's look again at our cosmic hierarchy, ranging from galaxies to quarks (or is it Higg's bosuns?) with oneself the human being stuck or set up in the thick of it, slap bang in the middle of her or his treble trouble. Where in this multi-level Cosmos shall we find the Cosmic Pharmacy, the recipe for our treble trouble? Has Douglas left anything essential out of his picture, any level where the magic medicine could be lurking?

What I'm now going to do, taking my cue from that excellent and well-known picture-book *Powers of Ten*, is to travel the cosmic hierarchy, starting beyond the galaxies, with Douglas here as the specimen I'm making for. I'll tell you about the scenery en route, while you check it against the illustration on p.22.

At first I find nothing, just boundless empty space. Then a number of tiny points of light appear. I approach one of them, and it grows bigger and brighter and is replaced by a fast-growing spiral of light. By a galaxy, which in turn is replaced by a vast collection of stars. Presently all but one of them vanish, and that one star is revealed as our Sun – a star which has developed into a solar system. Now the Sun vanishes and is replaced by the Earth, this beautiful planet. Homing in now on the planet, it's superseded in turn by a continent … a country … a town … a street … a building … a room, this room!

I've got you! I cry, and to prove it I whip out my Polaroid camera and take an instant snap of you … This snap. At which point Douglas interrupts vigorously. *Don't talk utter nonsense! You are at least eight feet short of me.* Way over there, you and your camera and my mirror have got Douglas all right, that froggy fellow who belongs half way down (and half way up) the cosmic hierarchy. In fact you are only half way along your journey. And if you want to find *me* waiting for you at journey's end you will have to come here where I am.

Catherine agrees. Resuming her journey to me, and taking further snapshots of what she finds on the way, she goes on with her story. I'm losing the lower half of my husband ... Now his torso's going ... I'm left with his face ... His eyes and nose and mouth are getting bigger and bigger ... and now they disappear ... leaving a patch of skin ... Which in turn disappears as I make contact ... Alas I've lost all trace of him. There's just a blur.

If I had been equipped with sophisticated cameras and the requisite optical and electronic microscopes and so on, this last stage of my journey to him would have been much more interesting. My tale would have run like this. The patch of skin, on closer inspection, turns out to be a huge gaggle of living creatures called cells. All of which proceed to vanish except for one of them, which on closer inspection turns out to be a very strange world of cell-organs and organelles, and then of complex and simpler molecules which have structure but no colour or life. Approaching just one of them, I lose it, and find instead atoms, then one atom, then particles, then just one particle. Which is just about next-door to nothing. In fact I've come to the disappointing end of my cosmic exploration. It looks as if the place where Douglas says he is is the place where he isn't, and I've widowed myself!

The reason for this unhappy anticlimax isn't hard to figure out. Following the example of *Powers of Ten*, I have neglected to ask my specimen to round off and complete my outside story of what he's made of, by telling his inside story. Which I now ask him to do. Knocking at his door, I shout: Is there anyone at home? What's it like in there, Douglas?

Pointing in to what he's looking out of, he replies: No outsider can make it to where I'm Nothing. I make it all the way. But if now, instead of looking in *at* me. you turn round and come here and look out *with* me, you will see and be the same conscious Nothing that I am, the Nothing that's capacious of Everything. (What other members of the workshop see at this point is Catherine and

Douglas putting their heads together while each holds out a world-embracing arm.) This Nothing-Everything is the Reality and the Source and the Centre of all those regional effects or appearances that Catherine came across on her long journey Home. Including, of course, that human object half-way.

The time has come for all the workshoppers to do among themselves what we have been doing, and to discover whether they come to the same or similar conclusions. Also to do another major experiment (such as the Tunnel or the Card), the aim of which is to see and take to heart the huge difference between what one is at Centre and what one looks like at a distance.

In ordinary therapy my disease is here and my medicine is over there. In the extraordinary therapy we are on about, my disease is there and my medicine is here. The rest of this workshop was spent discovering how perfectly fitted this central medicine is to the off-centre disease, how trebly effective against that treble trouble. Against our suprahuman lostness and meaninglessness, our human loneliness and strife and fear of death, our infrahuman conditioning and slavery.

That mid-way fellow is infinitesimal, his central Being is infinite. That mid-way one finds he's lost in the Universe, this central one finds the Universe is lost (or rather found) in him: he has room and to spare for any number of galaxies. The Point he points in to instantly explodes in all directions and beyond all limits. It's not that he believes or understands his capaciousness, but that he sees it even more clearly than he sees that little fellow's lack of it. In contrast to the puny arms of that fellow, these great arms visibly hold the Cosmos in a double embrace – the embrace of ownership and the embrace of love.

Now for our human level.

Out there we are all done up in separate parcels for early posting to Hell. Here at Centre we have nothing to keep one another out with. Here in Heaven each disappears in favour of the other. We don't work up feelings of love, but cease resisting the fact that we are busted wide open for one another, are built for loving.

That little chap is certainly built closed up, which means built for dying, and so is everything else. Every *thing* perishes. But at Centre you are No-thing and imperishable – the No-thing which is everywhere and all-embracing and wide, wide awake. Neither Death nor the fear of Death can get to where there's nothing to die. Nor can Death and the fear of Death get to *Things-as-a-Whole*. This Cosmos, this splendid Hierarchy of perishing wholes and parts that Catherine explored, is an indivisible and indestructible Totality. And this Totality is one's real Body, that Organism of which all bodies are organs, that One Life in virtue of which all lives live. Don't tell me that this real Body which we all share is messy or bedraggled or unlovely! If you can conjure up a more elegant and splendid and ageless and indeed heavenly physique, we would like to hear about it.

At this point someone asked how living consciously from our True Centre can get the better of physical pain. Douglas said that, compared with Catherine, he's a physical coward, and she's the one to answer this important question. She replied: I've suffered from arthritis for years, particularly in my hands, and recently from headaches. And I find that the pain, though by no means abolished, is subtly transformed. In fact there has to be a big difference when it's coped with from Where I am by the One I am, rather than by Catherine where she is. The way to discover that difference is to come Home and see for yourself .

Now what about the third of our treble troubles – the fivefold conditioning imposed on us by our ingredients which are our bosses, the infrahuman slavery? Well, there's just one region, one organ in our Whole Body that's absolutely free of all conditioning, that none of those bosses can get at. And that is where there's

Nothing to get at, no-one to boss. Here at the very Core and Mainspring of your Body is absolute freedom, for the simple reason that (rather cleverly!) you are altogether absent from the Place you are altogether present in! A trick guaranteed to baffle any slave-driver! In short, as What you are Where you are, you are Freedom itself.

Here, then, is our promised happy ending. You are the treble Cure for your treble trouble. Can you imagine a Medicine more nicely fitted to the Disease, more accessible, less subject to iatrogenic side effects or to overdose, more healing? Or a Medicine more underrated and under-prescribed.

It's for us to take the Medicine, and discover just how searching and comprehensive and cumulative are its effects. I know of no occasion or activity which will not benefit radically from large doses. And after all it's no surprise that what's done consciously by the one I am at Centre is going to be much better done than by the one I look like to you out there. Catherine and I aren't denying that this regimen is difficult, but we do add that, in our experience, such alternatives as exist are going to prove even more difficult in the long run.

All of us, even the healthiest, need this Medicine. As luck would have it, we live in what truly is, at basement level, a Pharmaceutical Universe. Or even a Sacramental Universe. But in that case (if I may adapt Coventry Patmore's lines):

> *How spoiled the Bread*
> *and spilled the Wine*
> *that tasted where there's none who tastes,*
> *had made brutes men*
> *and men divine.*

THE
CLOVERLEAF
JUNCTION

The editors of that invaluable magazine *Which?* are unlikely, in the foreseeable future, to bring out an issue on how to choose, not this time your car, or your camcorder, or your career, but your *spiritual* career, or Way Home. So it's up to us to tackle the job, however sketchily and briefly to outline the options with their pros and cons, their cost, and so on.

Consider the facts. Most intelligent and responsible young people devote time and care to considering what "worldly" career to take up, before committing themselves. They weigh the advantages against the disadvantages of different callings. They take advice. They may even try out some of the options, testing the temp-erature of the vocational bathwater before jumping in. Few stumble by accident or negligence into the thick of a lifelong career. But how different if and when those same intelligent and responsible young people come to what's immeasurably more important, to choosing their *spiritual* profession! They were pitchforked into it, by what bore all the marks of blind chance. A friend had a friend who had a ticket for that fascinating lecture. You were bullied and cajoled into reading that bombshell of a book. There was that charmer you picked up on the train: in fact she picked you up, and bagged another disciple for her beloved guru. You were bored and at a loose end, and that flaming circular fluttered onto your doormat, almost setting it alight. Or maybe you just dreamily slid into the faith of your fathers, as determined by their geography and social class and standard of living. And so on and on. Whatever it happened to be that launched you on your spiritual journey, I bet it wasn't in your case a careful study of the spiritual terrain, together with the roads traversing it and their respective traffic conditions, any more than it was in my case. Far from it!

Well, it's not too late to mend our ways. No matter how seasoned or unseasoned the traveller along any highway, or where he has or hasn't got to, the more he learns about road conditions ahead the better. Visibility, weather conditions, traffic flow, accidents, roadworks, and notice of diversions – it's neither safe nor sensible to turn a blind eye or deaf ear to whatever roadside or radio instructions are forthcoming. This is specially important if it's the spiritual road, the Homeward path that you and I are travelling. Hence this inquiry.

At this point you may tell me that your commitment to a particular spiritual path was not, in fact, determined by chance. It was determined by your temperament. Some of us are naturally drawn to the pursuit of Truth, others to the pursuit of Goodness, yet others to the pursuit of Beauty. Or maybe, if you are drawing on Eastern tradition, you will point out how widely our spiritual endowment or karmic heritage varies: with the result that few of us gravitate to the way of Knowledge, of the Sage or Seer, many to the way of Devotion, of surrender to God or to one of His or Her special incarnations or representatives, and a certain number to the way of Good Works, of selfless service to a suffering world. "Let me be true to my calling", you add, "to my talents (such as they are) and they will eventually take me Home. I travel my own road and mind my own business, recognising that the other travellers take other roads and drive other makes of vehicle that are probably running on other grades of fuel. Good luck to them!"

A plausible argument, but one I find unconvincing – for two reasons. First, I have to say that this appeal to my temperament or disposition or character means little to me. I don't know about you, but I can't be sure whether I'm the intellectual type, or the sensory-sensual type, or the emotional type, or the active type, or the bone-lazy type, or a pavement artist manqué, or (by the grace of God) some kind of alert idiot. What's more, no outsider is in a position to tell me. My inside information is that, if I have a temperament at all, it's a witch's brew consisting of all these ingredients and more, and which of them happens to surface depends on who's stirring the cauldron at the time. My second – and main – reason runs like this. Though it's certainly possible to get Home by one route alone, my stay there is very brief indeed, my visit at best a flying visit. In fact I shall be maintaining, later on in this chapter, that to get Home and enjoy Home and feel at Home one must arrive by a number of different routes. So that ultimately one's approach must be lateral and not merely linear, a convergence from all sides instead of a one-directional drawing near. From this it would follow that one's so-called temperament is an imagined restriction for growing out of rather than a real idiosyncrasy for cultivating.

Or perhaps (and surely with better reason) instead of invoking the phantom of temperament, you interpret the "chance happening" which started you off on your spiritual path as not a chance happening at all, but as the wise dispensation of a kindly and all-seeing Providence. In that case, I suggest that this same Providence (who is surely the All-rounder *par excellence* and the Prince of Broadmindedness and by no means choosy about ways Home to Himself) will heartily welcome your discovery of just how your special God-given way is so linked with the other special God-given ways Home that together they constitute one indivisible traffic system, a single influx or Homing. As we shall presently see.

In any case, these are the four options we shall be examining.

Route 1 – The Way of the Seer

The way of the Observer of What's Given, of What's True, whose journey Home to the Centre of All things is the same as his journey Home to his own Centre.

Route 2 – The Way of the Devotee

The way of self-forgetting Love, of those whose journey Home is to the Divine Other Who alone is for surrendering to.

Route 3 – The Way of the Servant

The way of the doer of Good, who makes for Home incidentally (so to say) by helping others to move in that direction.

Route 4 – The Way of the Artist

Whose way Home is a search for and creation of and dedication to the Beautiful.

Route 1: The Way of the Seer
Advantages

Of all routes Home this is by far the straightest, the most direct, the fastest, and there's no speed limit in either direction. The only rule of the road (and it's a must) is that you go by what you see and not by hearsay. The going is good and the traffic very light indeed. And for all who go this way it's the obvious way, and they are astonished it should be so unpopular.

To see just how obvious it is, how direct and fast, please make this journey of journeys right now. The illustration shows you what to do, but doesn't let you off doing it.

Hold out at arm's length a hand-mirror and take a fresh look at the face you see in there. Carefully observe how distant it is, how small, how complicated, how opaque, how packed full of itself to the exclusion of all others; not to mention how brief, how here today and gone tomorrow.

Well, that's what you are for yourself and

28

for others out there in the far country, a long way from Home.

Now, with the aid of your pointing forefinger, make this journey of journeys slowly and with due care and attention along the highway of your outstretched arm, all the way from your wrist to your elbow, and all the way from your elbow to your shoulder, and all the way from your shoulder to – *what?*

Surely to what, *on present evidence*, is the *absence* of neck, of adam's apple, of chin, of everything. To the No-thing, to the immense Space, to the Wide-Awake (repeat Wide-Awake) Emptiness or Clarity, to the welcoming Openness that greets you at journey's end.

Of all homes yours is on the grandest scale. Could the contrast between the Palace you are looking out of at the near end of your arm, and the what-shall-I-call-it? you are looking at at the far end, be any greater than it is, or more consistently overlooked than it is? What's more, the premises fit their occupants. For God's sake and for your sake and for all our sakes check that you are here and not over there, and that here at Home you see that you are perfectly at large, perfectly transparent, perfectly open, perfectly deathless.

Yes, your way Home by Route 1 is that easy, that obvious, that fast, that rewarding! And let me assure you – cross my heart – that this arm-trip was no armchair excursion, no imitation or preview or inferior version of your journey Home. Provided you bothered to fish out your mirror, and travelled with due care and attention and an open mind, this was the real thing and it took you all the way.

But in that case why is it so unpopular, so little travelled?

Disadvantages

Well, there are several reasons, several drawbacks (real as well as imaginary), several more-or-less-specious excuses for avoiding Route 1 like the plague, or even erasing it from the map altogether.

The first and foremost reason isn't far to seek, and we have already touched on it. You have probably noticed that the boundless clarity that your shoulder fades into was the briefest of glimpses. In fact you may already have asked yourself: why bother to travel anywhere if you aren't allowed to stop there long enough to look around, much less park? The truth is that only after many such flying visits are you granted a parking ticket. Which, understandably, few travellers are patient and persistent enough to earn.

The second reason for the unpopularity of Route 1, of the way of the Seer, is equally cogent and ready to hand. The trouble is that the road traverses such uninteresting country, such a boringly dull landscape, bleak and grey. Tell me, were you excited, thrilled, uplifted by your hand-to-no-mouth trip? Wasn't it downhill all the way? You and I read so much about the delights and consolations of the spiritual path – of any spiritual path worthy of the name. How many of those delights, how much of that wonderful consolation did you enjoy on that briefest and least thrilling of journeys? Or are likely to enjoy if you go on repeating it for ever and a day, like some demented Euroshuttle enthusiast who's hooked on the view along the Tunnel?

I should like at this point to add, for my part, a third snag to our list. Half a century spent observing travellers along this Seeing way – including myself, of course – has persuaded me of one thing. Namely, how all-too-easy it is to get Home quite regularly by this route and still fall distressingly short of the self-abandonment and humility and active compassion – to say nothing of enjoyment of the beauty that's everywhere – which would surely be ours if only we stayed at Home long enough to give them a chance. As it is, we seers are demonstrably no saints. Indeed, my impression is that, sooner or later, each one of us is going to find himself or herself to be worse and not better than the average decent human being! In that case, what price spirituality now? you may well ask.

That's bad enough, but the fourth disadvantage of Route 1 is worse, and by far the most off-putting of them all. The journey may well have left you fearful, or even frightened out of your wits, rather than fulfilled. And no wonder. Granted that the you that keeps cropping up in your mirror is a bad lot and defective in a thousand respects, and is in fact a convicted criminal awaiting execution – granted all that, at least that you *exists*, however briefly. At least there's *something* to you, however puny. At least you are *somebody*, never mind how lonely and lost and unloved among the billions of equally unfortunate somebodies. But even this spark and flicker of comfort goes up in smoke at the end of Route 1. I ask you and you ask me: what the blazes is the good of persistently and painstakingly making for Home, only to find that one has disappeared *en route*? What sort of welcome Home is it that finds nobody to welcome? Talk about the risks of travelling by road nowadays! Here's a highway that's *guaranteed* lethal!

All told, a formidable indictment. However I'm delighted to assure you that there's a radical answer to this line-up of objections. What's more, Route 1 itself conducts us to it, where it takes the form, familiar to drivers, of a cloverleaf junction – in this instance at least a truly lucky cloverleaf.

Let me put the matter picturesquely. Major roadworks and piled-up accidents and atrocious weather conditions not infrequently block the home stretch of Route 1. *The result is that I'm diverted onto one of the other three ways Home, via the cloverleaf.* The truth is, of course, that these not unusual sorry-for-the-delay hold-ups turn out to be a blessing in disguise. They ensure that my linear way Home develops laterally, that my one-sided approach becomes a convergence from all sides. The persistent seer isn't so much thrust as eased into devotion, into loving service, into loveliness. So that at last the words of the Mundaka Upanishad apply to him: "Having approached from everywhere that which is everywhere, whole, he passes into the Whole." No credit to the traveller. That's the set-up. Then and only then is he issued with unlimited parking tickets for use at the City Centre itself. And at last he's in a position to realise that here, and only here, is his perfecting, his incomparable safety, and how ridiculous all those fears of annihilation were.

In summary, then, whatever your chosen or unchosen way Home, do please give Route 1 a fair trial, for the following good reasons. It's economical and direct and fast and in good repair, and in the end it can't be bypassed. But don't expect too much of it unless and until you have travelled it so frequently that the varying road conditions (by which I mean the hitches and hold-ups that life is always confronting us with) have ensured that you have frequently travelled Home by the other routes also, notably by Route 2. And discovered what God means when He says to you, as to Al Niffari, "Satisfy Me as to thine eye, and I will satisfy thee as to thy heart."

Route 2: The Way of the Devotee

Advantages

The Homeward journey by this route, which is the Way of the Heart, contrasts sharply in almost all respects with the journey by Route 1, which is the Way of the Eye. Route 1 was cool, at times ice-cold – this is comfortably warm, at times piping hot. That was the contemplation of a Void, a Vacuum, an Absence that's no more exciting, or adorable, or colourful, or beautiful, or fragrant than a hole in your sock – this is a feeling that's not only rose-tinted and rose-scented but frequently rose-beautiful, a lovely loving that's poured out on an altogether loveable Being or Person or Superperson. That was a stern exercise in self-reliance, the taking oneself to no outside refuge that the Buddha strongly recommen-ded – this is self-surrender, a relaxed handing over to and leaning back with a sigh of relief on One you know will never let you down. That was a solitary and lonesome routine – this is a joyride with a bus-load of cheery fellow-devotees. And of course there's nothing so catching, so immediately barrier-demolishing, as the communal adoration of the same Divine Someone – whether that Someone happens to be the One Itself, or (more likely) some very special manifestation of or stand-in for that One.

Certainly, then, it's no surprise that Route 2 should be so much more popular than Route 1. And it's not only busy but obligatory. To some degree *en route*, and to the nth degree on arrival Home from whatever direction, your personal and superficial will has to be subordinated to the will of the One you really, really are. Only when you have no personal agenda, only when you have NOTHING TO DECLARE at Heaven's custom barrier, are you let in for good.

Disadvantages

In fact, this surrender of your personal will is the toughest and most exacting requirement imaginable. It's so demanding that, out of the huge numbers that set out on this road, and the considerable numbers who get a fair way along it, few arrive at journey's end and stop awhile. And so it happens that the final stretches of this road are no more travelled than those of Route 1. Rather less so, perhaps.

Moreover there lurk two formidable hazards along the way. The first is the risk that the adored Master may be exposed as quite unworthy of respect, to say nothing of adoration. After all, in claiming (or failing to disclaim) such a title as Sat-guru (Sanskrit for *Divinely Inspired Teacher*), or Maharaj (Sanskrit for *Great King*), or Swami (Sanskrit for *The Lord*), or Bhagwan (Sanskrit for *God*), or one or other of our less high-flying Western equivalents, he is indeed setting a high standard for himself, if not asking for trouble. And if it should transpire that his whole life has been a denial of the values he has insisted on, then to the dismay of his disciples is added the public scandal and the resulting denigration of spirituality in general. I'm not saying that this normally happens, but that it does happen. Devotees beware!

The second hazard is that, even if the Master disclaims that title and is no power-seeker, there's still a high risk that the disciple's devotion to him personally will prove so addictive that it stops with him. One might almost say that the less personable the Master the better, because the less likely to hold the disciple up a long way short of God. (I am thinking of St John of the Cross and St Vincent de Paul, neither of whom radiated saintliness.) It's all very well for the Master to insist (one hopes with perfect sincerity), "If you aren't willing or aren't ready to surrender to God, at least surrender to me, as a first step towards that true goal of all devotion." Too often it has proved the *last* step in that direction, and the poor disciple is stuck on the roadside indefinitely, a long way from Home. Probably stuck, if he's a Christian, in an idolatrous worship of the human Jesus – heedless of his warning that only God is good, addressed to the man who was rash enough to call him 'Good Master'. This title, please note, falls a long way short of Maharaj or Great King, to say nothing of Bhagwan or God. J.J.Ollier – a highly regarded spiritual director of the sixteenth century – had good reason to say "(Even) the sight of Jesus in his humanity can be an impediment to the sight of God in His purity."

But I must hasten to repeat that, in spite of these dicey road conditions and travel risks, this is a road we all have to travel in the end, to the end. And there the ultimate surrender is ours for taking on and merging in and surrendering to, and emphatically not for achieving. In Christian language, it is none other than partici-pation in the Divine Procession of Persons, in the Father's adoration of Himself as *other* than Himself, as the Son. And conversely, participation in the Son's worship of Himself as *other* than Himself, as the Father. Yes, indeed! Self-worship is no more sweet-smelling in God than in man. In truth, only God has no whiff about Him of that sickly odour. Only in Him who is Love itself is our love undiluted with self-love.

Route 3: The Way of the Servant

Advantages

This would seem to be a comparatively safe and uncontroversial Way Home. In fact, the average well-informed and well-behaved citizen will tell you that it's the only Way, the other Ways (insofar as they appear at all on the map) tending to morbid self-preoccu-pation and self-centredness. To feed the hungry, clothe and house and educate the poor, heal the sick – this is the true life of the Spirit, which consists of overlooking yourself and your private welfare in your care for others. And of course they have a point. The so-called spirituality that excludes others and is unmoved by their plight is a fake and a fraud. In Christian terms again, the leprous beggar is Christ travelling incognito, and anything you can do for him is done for Christ in Christ's own spirit, which cares more for him than for all the spiritual one-up-manship in Christendom.

Disadvantages

Again, if this is your only Way, you are pretty sure to run into trouble and get held up a long way from Home. While it's true that none of us can afford to bypass this road, none of us can afford to blind ourselves to its difficulties and dangers. Here are three of them.

To be a dedicated and unselfconscious do-gooder out of pure compassion, without any congratulatory casting of yourself in that saintly role, is mighty difficult. No! It's impossible! Was even St Vincent that holy, to say nothing of Mother Teresa? I can't see anyone getting Home on this ticket alone. It has to be combined with other tickets, other ways. With Route 1, for instance, where the safeguard against the traveller's self-congratulation is the disappearance of anyone to congratulate. Not that the recipient of your charity gives a tinker's cuss for your precious motivation, of course. And yes of course, better a charity that pats itself on the back a little, or even a lot, than no charity at all.

Along with the problem of mixed motives goes the problem of mixed consequences. What about the unkind consequences of your kindest acts, the unforeseen side-effects of your most effective remedies? Notoriously, short-term help has a nasty way of issuing in long-term hindrance. To help the helpless to cease needing your help – this is help indeed, but it's neither easy nor very common.

Finally and most importantly, there remains the question of what grade or level of help is truly helpful. Material and even psychological service, without regard to its spiritual results, can amount to the gravest disservice. I'm thinking of those 'rice-Christians' whose conversion by well-meaning missionaries was worse than worthless. And of the coma-inducing pain-killers administered so generously to the dying, with the result that the Homecoming that could have been the crowning adventure of the patient's life is shrouded and obliterated in dense fog. In short, to give your patient or your pauper what he wants, regardless, is no safer than to give your child what he wants, regardless; while to give him what you think he needs can be disastrous. Torquemada burned thousands of heretics alive because he believed it was good for their souls, in that it might at the last minute save them from everlasting fire.

What to do? How to discover what a person *actually needs*? The problems that one runs into along Route 3 are beginning to look so insoluble that you may well wonder whether it's a huge sidetrack and no Way Home at all.

But not to worry, kindly souls. There *is* a safeguard against the unforeseen and unforeseeable bad consequences of your good deeds, as well as the other drawbacks of this Way Home. It doesn't consist of nice calculations of probable results, or in any other kind of cleverness and taking thought. You'll not be surprised to hear that it is to supplement this Route 3 journey Home by combining it with frequent journeys there by other routes also, in particular Route 1. And this is how you go about it.

While looking in to see What you really are Where you really are, look out to see what you then get up to, quite naturally. Don't keep on asking why you are behaving as you are, or try to foresee all its consequences. Cease turning a blind eye to your Single Eye, which is the Eye of the One Who Sees. Cease overlooking the Central Stillness that moves all things, not least your alms-giving hands and gospel-bearing feet. And cease turning a deaf ear to the Central Silence that speaks with your comfort-bringing and inspiring voice. Do those things, and the rest shall be added. Do those things and remain assured that you are doing the right thing at the right time for the right people, notwithstanding appearances to the contrary. You may respond generously to that newly formed charity, or you may not. Wait and see, see and wait. You won't be kept waiting for long. Life at Home doesn't run by rules. It's a bus, not a tram, a free-as-the-air helicopter, not a road-bound bus. It is that only true and truly caring Spontaneity which is determined neither by habit nor by principle, but proceeds directly from the Origin of all things to the Solution of the problems It is continually coming up with. The know-what-to-do and the know-how-to-do-it arising from your divine Centre are infinitely wise and wonderful, while their analogues purporting to arise from your all-too-human periphery are illusory and in fact non-existent.

But don't believe me. Try trusting the former and distrusting the latter, from this day forth and for evermore.

Route 4: The Way of the Artist

Advantages

This Way Home is so little recognised in what you might call spiritual circles that you are probably surprised that I have included it at all. Well, by way of explanation, here's a true story.

The Curé d'Ars, canonised as St Jean-Baptiste Vianney, is among the most supernaturally gifted and appealing of modern saints. Yet when one of his parishioners brought him a beautiful red rose he turned sharply away, lest it should divert him from the Divine Beauty. For the Curé, "the lust of the eyes" like "the lust of the flesh" constituted a devilish setback on the way Home and by no means a divine push in that direction. I suspect that this unhappy one-sidedness was linked with the twin facts that, like Padre Pio, he engaged in many horrific bouts with the Devil in person, and also found it necessary to flagellate himself at regular intervals. Two uglinesses that might have been avoided if only he had seen that all beauty – not least that of the flesh – witnesses to and stems from the Beauty of the One he so passionately adored. It's a pity that, lacking a liberal education, he probably never read Plato's *Symposium*, in which Socrates, with matchless charm and eloquence, shows how the enjoyment of beautiful Earthly forms can and should lead one by stages to the enjoyment of Beauty itself, laid up in Heaven.

But here you may feel like siding with the French priest rather than with the Greek philosopher, in denying that – or at least doubting whether – the pursuit of Beauty necessarily leads one Homewards. After all, those successful pursuers Toulouse Lautrec and Paul Gauguin and Pablo Picasso (to mention just three Modern Masters) along with the majority of Old Masters, were neither saints nor sages. Nor, for that matter, do Shakespeare or Dante or Rembrandt or Mozart run any risk of canonisation. Nevertheless I

37

must insist that the star-studded galaxy of genius in the fine arts provides a priceless and indispensable service to us all, and moreover does so with the utmost dedication and despite the high personal cost. In our terms, though innocent of any such intention, they combine travelling by their own Route 4 with travelling by Routes 2 and 3. And I don't doubt that the most gifted of them all (including Meister Eckhart and St John of the Cross and Rumi, who were literary as well as spiritual Masters) travelled by Route 1 also, by the Seeing Way. Shakespeare, at least, did so with full consciousness: witness his warning in *Measure for Measure* that we are in danger of behaving like angry apes just so long as we persist in overlooking our 'glassy essence' - alias our Central Transparency.

At this juncture you may remind me that few of us are masters of any art, let alone great masters. True, but this doesn't mean that Route 4 is closed to us ordinary mortals. Not at all. Here's another true story that illustrates my point.

Way back in 1964, I conducted what amounted to a Seeing Workshop at a Buddhist Summer School near London. Among those present who 'saw' was a gentleman who introduced himself as Lt.-Col. Roger Gunter-Jones. Walking with me next day in the garden, he was astonished at the brilliance of certain roses, and wondered what country the bushes had been imported from. But as we moved on to look at other flowers he discovered that they were just as startlingly beautiful. It was just as if all the colours in Roger's world had suddenly burst into song. And there's a pleasing sequel to this tale. Down the road from the Summer School there festered an ill-concealed and ill-smelling corporation rubbish dump. And here, later in the week, I chanced on Roger staring intently into the mess of old cans, broken furniture and crockery, and crumpled and filthy newspapers. There he stood, entranced by the visible rightness and inevitability of the colours and patterning of all that was on show, the sheer perfection of it all. Not at all the sort of behaviour or sentiment you would expect from a retired regular-army officer and embassy attaché!

The truth is that when, as part of our growing up, we make the monstrous but mandatory mistake of superimposing that head-in-the-mirror upon our own shoulders here (instead of leaving it out there where it fits nicely on other shoulders) it obscures and dulls and distorts all that we see. And the only way to rediscover the deliciously bright and shining world we lost when we grew up is to turn our attention round to What's in receipt of it all at this very moment, and see that right here there remains not so much as a dust-grain in the way of all that overlooked glory. I grant you, of course, that this childlike enjoyment of the world is very different from celebrating it in great compositions of words or paint or sound. But it is great after its own fashion, and - yes! - profoundly creative, and by no means the passive affair you might mistake it for. And in the end it's a *must*, if you would take up residence in the Palace of Beauty itself.

So if you happen to be a dedicated practitioner of one or other of the fine arts - a traveller, that is, by Route 4 - allow yourself to be diverted onto other routes and specially onto Route 1, as often as may be. You will then become a still better artist, one who sees what he or she's up to. Or, if you consider yourself no artist, I say to you: like Roger, include Route 1 in your itinerary and you will find that you *are* an artist enjoying union with the Artist Who at the world's Centre is busy creating an incredibly beautiful scene - rubbish dumps, and stains on old walls, and leaves littering garden paths, and so on ad infinitum.

You may have noticed that I haven't managed, so far, to find any built-in snags comparable with those that afflict the other three ways Home. Our assessment of Route 4 has consisted pretty much of pros rather than cons. This is significant if not surprising, and one of the best reasons for giving it an honourable place in our roundabout, our lucky cloverleaf junction. The worst thing I can think of to say about Route 4 is that its users are apt to give themselves and sometimes those around them a hard time. Like Mozart, for instance. So what? His music tells me something essential about God, and the Universe, and myself, that can be told in no other way, in no other language, by no other human being.

Conclusion: The Cloverleaf Junction

Our job is to box the compass, to allow ourselves to ripen into all-rounders, each in his or her own fashion. God forbid that we should take the famous Indian sage Ramakrishna (1836-86) for our model, but he does provide a fascinating and revealing instance of all-rounding. At six years of age (*six*!) he was so overcome by the beauty of white birds flying in a storm-dark sky that he passed out for hours; and till the end of his short life a snatch of music or a chance patterning of forms and colours was liable to have the same effect. At twenty, he became the priest of a temple dedicated to Kali, the black Mother of the Universe who creates with one hand and destroys with the other. Ramakrishna's devotion to the Deity in this striking form was absolute. But at length there arrived at the temple a naked sadhu called Tota Puri. To accomplish the difficult task of weaning Ramakrishna from Mother Kali to the Formless God, Tota Puri stuck a sliver of glass in the young priest's forehead and told him to meditate on that. This time he passed out for days, and emerged as the devotee of Kali no longer, but of the nameless ineffable Source of all. The Devotee had become the Seer. So much, in our terminology, for his pursuit of Routes 4 and 2 and 1. What of Route 3, the Way of Works, of Service? Well, the distinctive feature of the community of monks that Ramakrishna founded, is none other than loving service, in all sorts of practical ways, to a suffering world. So the compass was boxed, the wheel turned full circle, the moving spokes converged on the still Hub.

When I was young there was a popular song entitled *Show Me The Way To Go Home*. I think it was sung by Stanley Holloway, who was playing drunk at the time. I'll say this for him, however, though intoxicated, he had the right idea. Most of us are so blind drunk that we don't realise how far from Home we have wandered. Unlike stray dogs we are unaware that we are strays. We are so drunk that we take Home to be the crumbling box we creep into at night. And a lot of us who do make for our true Home are so tipsy that we imagine there's only one way there – namely, of course, *our* way! Well, let's sober up and, making full use of our lucky cloverleaf, converge on Home from all sides, arrive Home, enjoy Home, and at last take up residence in the Palace we never really left.

5

THE TRIDENT

The previous chapter described four ways Home to the Place we never really left – the Way of the Seer, of the Devotee, of the Servant and of the Artist. But there are other important routes that can take us some of the way there, even most of the way. I'm referring, in particular, to Science and Religion. To the Science that includes the sciences and the Religion that includes the religions and the varieties of religious experience.

This illustration shows how these two additional routes fit into our traffic system.

They are linked with and feed into Route 1, the Way of the Seer. In this chapter we shall be finding out just how far Science and Religion can take us would-be seers towards our goal and how much easier they can make our approach.

Towards what goal? I can hear someone asking. The short but unhelpful answer is: to a goal that can't be clearly conceived – much less perceived and enjoyed – until we arrive there.

The longer and more encouraging answer is: to a goal that may provisionally be pencilled in as the discovery of the meaning of our life and all life, as the clear vision of What we really are Where we really are, as freedom from fear and greed and hate and delusion, as the uncovering and tapping of our inmost resources, as the attainment of peace, as conscious union with our Source, as Homecoming. Of necessity such speculative previews of this Goal of goals are many and complicated, wordy and mist-shrouded. They amount to a bunch of tasty carrots dangled before the donkey's nose to urge him on. The Reality – a more nourishing fare that somehow includes all the vitamins I've just listed (it has been called the Living Bread and the very Wine of Life) – is one and simple and wordless, as we shall see.

I aim to show how serviceable, how well-fitted to our purpose, these two additional routes can be, and how our Seeing Way is their needful re-routing and reconciling and merging with each other, so that all three arrive Home with banners flying. Let's start, then, with

The Way of Science

The Cosmos is a big country in which we easily get lost. And the special gift that Science hands us is a comprehensive and sufficiently detailed map of the Way Home.

It points the way down from the human being to what he consists of, to his cells, molecules, atoms, particles – to his ingredients, to what's in him. Also it points the way up to what he's part of – the Planet Earth, the Solar System, the Galaxy – to his milieu, to what he's in. We have here a hierarchy in which each is a part of the wholes above it and the whole of the parts below it. Read downwards, it pulls everything to pieces to see what it's made of. Read upwards, it puts them together again to see what they make up.

Let's now look at the map rather differently. To the un-prejudiced observer who is approaching me from far, far away, I first appear as this luminous spiral we call our Galaxy, then as one of its stars (our Sun, which is a developed star, a solar system), then as one of its planets, then as one of its inhabitants, and so on down to the realm of particles and their constituent quarks.

For him I am all these regional appearances or manifestations of the mysterious Reality at the Centre that's giving rise to the whole astonishing display. And how happy and thrilled I am to thumb a lift and share his sight-seeing trip, travelling in with him to me. Or perhaps I should say: travelling in with him through me to Me.

There's yet another way to read this map of myself that Science so generously provides me with. It poses and answers such questions as: What does this human being *need* in order to be this human being, in order to be at all? What is he without his cellular population, without the billions of living creatures he turns out to be on closer inspection, that actually get down to the business of doing whatever he claims he's doing? And what is each of these humble but amazingly efficient servitors without the billions of molecular servitors that each cell turns out to be on still closer inspection? And so on down and down. Down to What? – that's half the question. And up to What? – that's the other half. What is this particular human being without Earth's other humans, without her air and water and soil and flora and fauna? How long could he survive without his Sun, or exist without his Cosmos? When he tells you he's alive (let alone quite well thank you) he's telling you, without realising it, that he's *the One whose life is* INDIVISIBLE.

Yes, it's a good map, responsive to the interests and needs of its users. How thankful we humans should be for this chart in all its details and varieties, this Guide Michelin to our astonishing Nature and Constitution! Five hundred years ago it was imposs-ible, a hundred and fifty years ago it was incomplete and optional, now it's indispensable.

But like all maps, of course, it has its omissions and limitations, and it can be misread and misused. Certainly it can be and is ignored. The astonishing truth is that almost nobody takes it seriously and to heart, and admits that it applies to himself *personally*. "It's valid for others, no doubt, but not for me" says Homo sapiens (so-called) in effect, without saying it. *He believes in science only insofar as it serves his unscientific needs and desires.* Take the following small sample of the many instances of his turning a blind eye to the facts. Though he has some rough text book knowledge of what happens in the womb, of the development of the embryo and foetus from the fertilized egg, does he ever grasp the fact that *in his own lifetime he was an almost invisible single cell, and hugely inferior in biological status to the cheese-mites he ate at lunch*? Or realise that even now he's a walking zoo consisting of the extended family of that original cell? Or appreciate that, on still closer inspection, he's less substantial than a cloud? Or get the feel that his Earth and Sun, *unlike his precious arms and legs, are absolutely necessary organs of his true Body*? The answer to these and a host of similar questions, is No! Not on your life! He's pre-scientific, at least five hundred years behind the scientific times. To prove it he will tell you, when faulted, that he's only human after all – a pronouncement that, for sheer goofiness, deserves an Olympic gold.

No wonder the traffic along Science's route towards our Goal, to the Truth that sets us free, is as light as it is.

There are two additional reasons for this neglect – reasons which, for a change, aren't goofy. The first is that this road ends as it began, with a question mark, as indicated on our map. It runs into difficult and foggy country. The traveller can photograph cells in great detail, and take passing snaps of beautiful and complex molecule-models. but when he comes to their atoms and particles, he finds a warning notice: *Keep out! Road closed to all but mathematising physicists.* Such news as filters through from these sequestered regions isn't reassuring. No physicist has the nerve to claim that at last he has unveiled for sure the ultimate Reason for and Ingredient of the Cosmic Concoction, the sub-sub-quark (or whatever) that all things are made of. The findings of these experts are worthy of respect but are never unanimous and always in the melting pot.

The second reason why the spiritual wayfarer (if I may call you and me that) is loath to take the Way of Science towards his longed-for Home, is historical. Science has a well-earned reputation as the enemy of religion. All its major advances have been hard-won victories over the religious Establishment's most cherished dogmas. As for its applications, at a guess a good half of them have been misapplications, the endless list of which ranges from Hiroshima to heroin, from junk food to junk mail telling us what we must now possess, and that will promptly go on to possess and enslave us.

No wonder that spirituality is wary of science. All the same I ask: what is pure science, apart from all its abuses and seen for what it is, but humility in front of the evidence, respect for the truth no matter how unflattering or shocking. Of its ethical value that least stuffy of philosophers William James wrote: "When one turns to the magnificent edifice of the physical sciences and sees how it was reared; what thousands of disinterested moral lives of men lie buried in its mere foundations; what patience and postponement, what choking down of preference, what submission to the icy laws of outer fact are wrought into its very stones and mortar, how absolutely impersonal it stands in its vast augustness, – then how besotted and contemptible seems every little sentimentalist who comes blowing his voluntary smoke-wreaths, and pretending to settle things from out his private dream. Can we wonder if those bred in the rugged school of science should feel like spewing such subjectivism out of their mouths?"

To which let us add: the spirituality that rubbishes the universally agreed findings of modern science at all levels, or refuses to face up to them and cheerfully take them on board, is a pathetic and moribund travesty of spirituality. And conversely, the spirituality that finds in them a rich and precious and indeed divine revelation of our time and for our time, and just what's needed to treat our sorry condition, is alive and kicking. Yes, this Way has become indispensable. It gets us, you could say, to a place where a distant view of our Home can occasionally be had, in calm and clear weather. Though it's silent about what that door opens onto it couldn't be more eloquent about its importance, and its whereabouts, and specially its power.

As we descend the Cosmic Hierarchy, loss of form means gain of power.

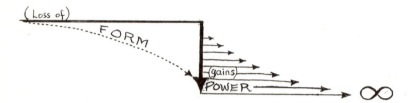

Cells pack a lot of energy at their own level, molecules more, but a TNT bomb is nothing like so powerful as an atomic bomb. Which in turn is nothing like so powerful as a nuclear bomb. These are dirty devices, of course, misapplications of science proper. But the Zero Bomb which is our true Goal is all-clean and all-powerful. It is this Goal of Goals that science on its own falls short of.

Its distant view of Home, shrouded in the rainbow mists of higher mathematics, is far from enough. We are bent on arriving. The question we must now address is: can religion succeed where science fails? Can it disperse those mists and clear the way to the door of Home? Does it hold the key to that door?

The Way of Religion

If we look for help here to what goes by the name of religion, to religion as a social phenomenon, to religion as described and practised by the majority of its adherents, to religion as dished out daily in the media, we shall surely look in vain. So far from clearing mists away, it piles up the pollution and obscurity. As for its history, religion has been responsible for more inhumanity, more pig-headedness, more fat-headedness, more terror, more fraud than any other human undertaking.

Yet here's a case of the worst concealing the best. Common to the world's great faiths is a Metaphysic – a wisdom, a spirituality, a secret and often cruelly suppressed teaching – according to which, in spite of all appearances to the contrary, you and I and all our fellow creatures are, at Centre, not creatures at all, but One with their Creator. That at the core of all beings lurks Being Itself, the Nameless One whose nicknames include Atman-Brahman, the Buddha, the Tao, God, the Indwelling Christ, the Holy Spirit, Allah, Reality, Consciousness, the No-thing that is Everything.

This Metaphysic gives us two priceless pieces of information about the Nameless One. We are told exactly *where* It is. And exactly *what* It is, exactly how we shall recognise It when at last we track it down.

According to Mohammed It's nearer to me than my neck-vein. According to Tennyson It's nearer than my breathing, closer than hands and feet. Much, much closer, say all those who know what they are talking about. The very spot I'm looking out of, the place I'm coming from, the Centrepoint that is far more Me than Harding is me – this is the Home, the royal palace of His Divine Majesty, say the world's great spiritual teachers. In fact, it's as if He had two palaces, a winter palace in the highest heavens and a summer palace deep in our hearts. And it's down here and right now, rather than up there and one fine day, that I must seek admission to His august presence.

So much for His whereabouts. Now for His whatabouts, His distinctive features. I must know what they are, and here's why. Supposing I said to you: "I've lost a treasure in the garden, but can't remember what it is. Please help me find it", you would surely laugh at me. By the same token I smile at people who look for God without a clue about what they are seeking. Happily, however, the Perennial Metaphysic, the secret wisdom that underpins the great religions, comes up with a remarkable composite portrait, a perfect six-sided identikit of His Divine Majesty. Here it is.

1. He's boundless
2. He's empty
3. and therefore imperishable
4. But empty for filling, all-inclusive
5. He's wide awake
6. He's the unmoved Mover of the world

Science gave us a wonderful map with, however, a teasing question mark at both ends of it. Now Religion has erased those question marks. It has given us a precise description of the Wonder that underlies the quark and overtops the galaxies. It has told us exactly how to recognise the Inhabitant of those summer and winter palaces. It couldn't be more specific. We can no longer pretend that we don't know what our lost treasure looks like, what we are seeking in the garden of the world. This is good news.

But even the best news about It isn't It. The specification, no matter how accurate and detailed, is no substitute for the building. The map isn't the territory, and even the best police identikit is incapable of hand-cuffing the culprit. You can learn all the holiest scriptures by heart, you can practise bodily and mental austerities till you are reduced to skin and bone, you can meditate on our six criteria till kingdom come, you can have faith by the bucketful – but all this is a million miles from seeing Him and being Him.

The truth is that religion, as such, is about faith and hope and charity, not the Beatific Vision. Its business is believing in and trusting the Invisible. We must have faith, says the Epistle to the Hebrews, in the things which are not seen. "For the things which are seen," says the Second Epistle to the Corinthians, "are temporal. But the things that are not seen are eternal." This doesn't mean, of course, that faith and hope and charity don't matter. Of course they do, immensely, but when they rule out vision I have problems. A bouquet of problems.

The first I have already touched on. It is that faith in and hope for the Real are no substitute for the Real, any more than chewing on the menu is a substitute for my dinner. The second is that, in my experience, while seeing is believing, believing isn't seeing. Believing is just believing, and subject to recurrent lapses and doubts and warning signals about wishful thinking. What I can doubt I will doubt, sooner or later. The ostensibly good things of religion come with high price-tags attached. The countless myths and tall stories and convoluted theologies and bizarre practices that are built into the great faiths can't, they say, be treated as optional extras, take them or leave them. My instinct is to leave them, with not too much regret. The last problem is the worst. Of all defences against the sight of What one is Where one is, religion is commonly the most formidable. Certainly it adds to the difficulties of my job. As a rule it is religious people – earnest and dedicated Christians and Buddhists and Muslims – who are most allergic to my message.

The Perennial Metaphysic, announcing the Godhead immanent in every one of us, shakes itself free from all religious traps and trappings, all accidents and irrelevancies, and stands clean and austere in its simple grandeur. Put bluntly, *the Perennial Meta-physic isn't religious at all.* Or let's say it's meta-religious, and very different from religion as generally understood and practised. In other words it isn't the religious way to our Goal. It's the Seeing Way. It's seeing what we see and daring to go by that, and not by what religion tells us to see and forbids us to see. It's that same uncompromising humility in front of the evidence that has given us pure science.

The Way of Seeing

The time has come for you and me to point – whether for the first or the umpteenth time – into What we are looking out of, and SEE whether it is:

1. Boundless
2. Empty
3. and therefore Imperishable
4. But empty for filling, All-inclusive
5. Wide awake
6. The Unmoved Mover of the scenery that people say you are moving through.

Provided you actually did the pointing and the looking to see what moves (and didn't just read about them) and provided you took seriously – took to heart – what you clearly saw, why then you saw your way Home, you made it all the way to the Goal we sketched in at the start of this chapter. And you have my heartfelt congratulations.

To which I must immediately add three caveats.

The first is that the vision is essentially matter-of-fact and unexciting. In sharp contrast to the famous but rare and un-predictable peak experiences enjoyed by some who follow the religious way, it's a valley experience, sober and profoundly humbling. And, just because it's for simply seeing and not for understanding and getting worked up about, it's there on demand, whatever one's mood or circumstances. Thanks to the fact that it's the very opposite of a mystical experience, it's most available when most needed.

Which brings me to my second caveat. You and I have, very briefly indeed, seen God, the six-sided One. Now we need to stabilise that vision. It was, while it lasted, the real thing and no amateurish or partial vision of Him Who is perfectly seen or not seen at all. However this is the beginning and not the end of the spiritual life. The vision has to be practised, practised, practised. But it's a practice that's enjoyment and no chore, and we have no excuse for neglecting it. We know where to look (namely, right here), and when to look (namely, right now), and how to look (namely, as if for the first time), and why to look (namely, because to miss this vision is to be a serious case of mistaken identity, to live and die in vain).

This brings me, in turn, to my third caveat. If we practise the Beatific Vision in order to reap one day its advertised benefits – peace, joy, love, freedom, creativity, and so on – we aren't likely to garner a rich harvest. Whereas if we do so for it's own sake and with no axe to grind, because living from the amazing Truth is a more attractive proposition and makes better sense than living from a pack of socially-dictated lies, why then we are much more likely to gain the unsolicited and unimaginable gifts that await us. All in God's good time. In fact, it is God Himself, not His bulging haversack of gifts, that is the real Gift, bestowed with infinite generosity.

It remains for me to add something about the Seeing Way as the rectification and reconciliation and completion of the Way of Science and the Way of Religion.

I once wrote a little book called *The Science of the First Person* about the seven or eight respects in which the Science of the First Person (which is another name for the Seeing Way) sheds light on the dark places of regular science. They promptly grew from seven or eight into thirty-seven! Rather than take my word for it, why not read it for yourself?

Both science and religion, in isolation from each other, are, as we have already seen, responsible for much human misery. Their diversion into the Way of Seeing and mutual rectification could only mean the alleviation of much of that misery.

It cannot but endorse and fulfil the faith and hope and charity, along with all the other good and beautiful things that traditional religion enshrines. It cannot but cleanse religion of mountains of accumulated rubbish, some of it stinking.

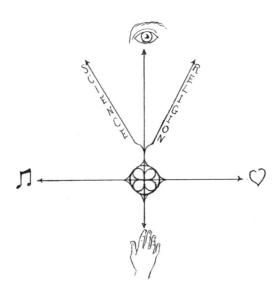

6

On Being Out
OF THE
Ordinary

If you have become a throne of God,
And the Heavenly Charioteer has mounted your chariot,
And your whole soul has become a spiritual eye
and totally light,
And if you have been nourished with the
heavenly food of the Spirit
And have drunk the water of Life,
And if you have put on the raiment of Light,
And if, finally, your interior man has experienced all these,
And has been rooted in the abundance of faith –
Then behold! you already live the Eternal Life,
And your soul is resting with the Lord!
Pseudo-Macarius (4th century, AD)

For itself, every creature is very special. In the cosmic ordering of things you have been appointed the sole and natural guardian of your own importance, your centrality, your uniqueness. This appointment, this sine-qua-non of existence, is for taking seriously and not for denying or brushing to one side. It's for facing up to and somehow coping with.

The trouble, of course, is that there are others – lots and lots of them – whose role seems to be the frustration and denial of your

53

importance and centrality and uniqueness. And how dedicated they are to the task! We humans are all-too-aware of this painful contradiction, this fundamental problem of oneself versus the rest. And we have come up with four ways of coping with it, which I shall call here the Way Up, the Way Down, the Up-and-Down Way, and the Way Through.

Let's take them in that order.

The Way Up

To win, to get the better of others by doing better than they do, to succeed by hook or by crook where they fail – this is an endeavour that none of us can avoid. To achieve something is to surpass someone, if a toy's mine it isn't yours, my winning a race means your losing it, my making a living is picking the public pocket. Only so, can I grow up and become a member of this highly competitive society that must be clear about who owns what.

This compulsive urge to win, to shine, to best the rest, to be a very special person amongst much less special persons, necessarily meets with much frustration and disappointment as we grow older. Sooner or later *Win some, lose some* becomes my motto, grudgingly. Only to be replaced, eventually, with the even more discouraging *Alas, I can't take it with me*. Even before Death the Leveller wins back all our winnings he lays a cold finger on them. Riches in any quantity and achievements in any field will never be enough to invest us with the importance that we feel is our due. Not nearly enough! To have and to hold what we have won gives little pleasure, to take care of it gives much trouble, while to lose it gives much pain. There really is a sense in which nothing fails like success.

Understandably, some people have drawn from this fact the conclusion that there really is a sense in which nothing succeeds like failure. They have chosen the Way Down.

The Way Down

This Way makes its case along the following lines. "Why bother to enter for the rat-race that I can never win? In fact I withdraw my pretensions to being a rat at all, let alone a special rat. I'm a nobody. No, this isn't Uriah (ever so 'umble) Heap speaking, but anyone who's practising any kind of moral or spiritual discipline worthy of the name. It has to include the very difficult cultivation of humility."

Not that this Way Down is for would-be saints only. To some extent it's for us unsaintly ones also. Flying the banner with the strange device *Excelsior*!, climbing relentlessly, insisting on always being the up-and-coming one – this is self-defeating, sick, and in the end fatal. In fact, just as we can't altogether avoid the Way Up, we can't altogether avoid the Way Down. Some of each is the price of sanity. Life sees to it that we alternate between them.

But in any case to practise humility deliberately is quite silly. Why should I do so? There's only one honest answer. Namely, to become specially humble, far humbler than you. Of course I'm much too humble to boast to you about it, but I can hardly avoid boasting to myself! No way can I help being proud of my humility! So far from relinquishing my claim to distinction and importance, I have with undiminished ardour sought it elsewhere – below instead of above – and moreover have done so with less candour and self-criticism. And the whole enterprise reveals itself as ridiculous. In fact, no saint practises humility as a separate exercise, apart from the One in whose presence all his pretensions go up in smoke anyway.

But this chapter and this book are about you and me, not about saints. About what I call up-and-down people.

The Up-and-Down-Way

Half the time, say, things happen the way I want them to happen, and I feel I'm winning the game of life. And half the time they happen the way I don't want them to happen, and I feel I'm losing the game of life. This yo-yo-like existence isn't a comfortable one, and results in much anxiety. My distress arises, of course, from my built-in conviction that I'm special and deserve to win, while the message coming from the others is that I'm not at all special and much of the time deserve to lose.

Uncomfortable and rickety though the set-up is, it creaks along after a fashion. Each effective member of a social group, of any sort of organisation or business, is secretly convinced of his special-ness and importance and indispensability, no matter how low his status, and his certainty makes its contribution to the group as a whole. If my job is sweeping the floor, the job and the way I do it and the state of the floor are all special. They revolve round the Centre that I am. But of course it's an up-and-down affair. Some days I hate it and do it badly, other days I don't. Rarely is it free from anxiety, from neurotic anxiety.

In addition to neurotic anxiety, as Harry Stack Sullivan pointed out, we suffer from another and more basic kind which he called existential anxiety. No matter how ignored or repressed, there lurks in us the knowledge that we are the briefest of specks in this immense Universe, that if our life has any meaning at all Death and Oblivion are poised to make nonsense of it, that our pretensions to centrality and importance are a bad joke. And so we muddle along, now up and now down, always haunted by the certainty of ultimate defeat, and subject in varying degrees to existential anxiety.

The good news is that there is, as we are about to see, a fourth way of coping with the human situation and its intrinsic anomalies and contradictions and resulting anxieties. Though it is a vast improvement on the others we don't come to it by ignoring or denying our human plight, but by admitting it in tones loud and clear.

The Way Through

Strictly speaking, what follows isn't so much *the way* as *a way through*. It is one of a number of solutions that are on offer, solutions to the problem of one's profound sense of uniqueness and centrality in a universe that seems dedicated to pooh-poohing it. But I hope you will find that (unlike some of the alternative through-routes) it is direct and clear of obstructions and well sign-posted, that the going's good throughout, and that it can get us all the way to our destination. Everything will depend on your willingness to conduct the following experiment. Never mind how often and successfully you have done it before, I must ask you to do it again – this time with a crucial difference.

You will need at least four friends, one of whom reads out the following instructions, and helps the others to comply with them conscientiously.

Experiment: part one

Each of you is supplied with a card with a head-sized hole in it, and a mirror that's roughly as big as the card.

Hold the card out at arm's length and note how *empty* that hole in the card is, how *imperishable* that space is (there's nothing there to perish), how *timeless* (there's nothing in it to register time with).

Now see how perfectly *filled* that space is with whatever's on show (with the opposite wall and window and curtains, plus your feet and legs, for instance), and how perfectly *united* that imperishable emptiness is with its contents, every one of which is perishing.

Observe, however, how this fullness-emptiness has three severe limitations. It's bounded by the card and quite small, it's over there and not here where you are, and it's unconscious.

Now overcome these three limitations by slowly and with total attention putting on the hole in the card as if it were a mask.

And, as you do so, watch for the moment of truth when (i) the card vanishes and the space in it explodes to infinity, (ii) the space is no longer distant but right where you are, and (iii) it wakes up in you and as you: so that the space you were looking at becomes the space you are looking out of, the empty and filled and boundless and imperishable space that is you, that you are.

And now, with your card held on as far as it will go, look round at your friends – your funny friends. See that, on present evidence, only you have left behind your humanness with its limitations, and

57

arrived at the limitless and timeless and imperishable fullness-emptiness that's alive to itself as the possessor of these essentially divine attributes. See how your friends are stuck in their cards, stuck with their humanhood, and only you are clean through to your Godhood.

And if all the sentient creatures in the Universe were to be crammed into your sitting-room, and each supplied with a holed card of appropriate design, and persuaded to carry out our experiment along with you, *you would still be the only one to jump clear of its little hidey-hole into the OPEN!* Every one of those marmot-like creatures would visibly be held up at the mouth of its hole, stuck with its own particular creatureliness. Yes, you are the Alone, the Absolutely Unique One! And your lifelong dedication to your specialness and centrality and importance was more than prophetic. It was perfectly justified, altogether well-founded, from the start!

End of experiment – part one.

And the beginning, I guess, of a serious doubt in your mind. I can hear you saying: "What's true for me must be true for each of the others, in his or her experience. There's nothing to prevent anyone breaking through to the other side of the card and claiming the

uniqueness that I claim. Obviously this uniqueness is nonsense, a subjective delusion. The ultimate delusion of grandeur, at that!"

Part Two of our Experiment addresses this objection.

With one hand hold your card right on, and with the other hand hold out your mirror at arm's length.

You'll not be surprised to see how that familiar person behind glass over there, a metre or so distant from where you are this side of the glass, is stuck, along with the myriads of other marmots, at the mouth of his hole. He's one of them, nothing out of the ordinary, not special at all!

But wait a minute!

See how, this side of the glass, you are still this unbounded and imperishable Space for things to happen in. Observe the total contrast between the human you that side of the glass and the Divine You this side, which is your side, the side you are on. Right here you are still absolutely out of the ordinary, absolutely unique.

How can these two wildly incompatible versions of you coexist?

The fact of the matter is that *no creature gets through to its divinity AS THAT CREATURE.* Unable to survive the rigours of that journey of all journeys, it perishes en route. Only the Special One gets through to the Special One. Only the Alone makes it all the way to the Alone. His amazing grace sees to it that you really are through to Him - *not as you but as Him.*

What you now have to do is to take up His invitation and go on seeing your way Home to Him till your seeing becomes much more than seeing. Till it ripens into trusting wholeheartedly the only One that's absolutely trustworthy, and merging whole-heartedly into the only One that can really be merged into. And then you will find that, as Sullivan suggests, the last traces of your neurotic anxiety will dissolve, because your basic existential anxiety - about your true Identity - is finally dissolved.

I don't know what other practical conclusions you draw from our experiment, but here are mine.

Though so slow to follow Part One of our experiment (it took me 37 years to do so), I found that Part Two turns out to be very important indeed. Seeing God in and Harding off are two inseparable halves of a single operation. No way can I have the one without the other. Until I firmly locate my humanness out there along with all the rest, until I hold it out there in my bare hands, there is always the risk of its creeping here and infecting my Divine Centre, reducing it to a horrendous - indeed devilish - delusion of grandeur. It's far from enough that I completely understand and deeply feel and believe in the unbridgeable gulf that separates my humanness from my divinity. I need to *see* it, and see it I do. How can I express my relief at this seeing-off, this cleansing, this unburdening, this sure salvation? To be saved is to *be Him*.

AT CENTRE YOU REALLY ARE OUT OF THE ORDINARY

INTO THE EXTRAORDINARY

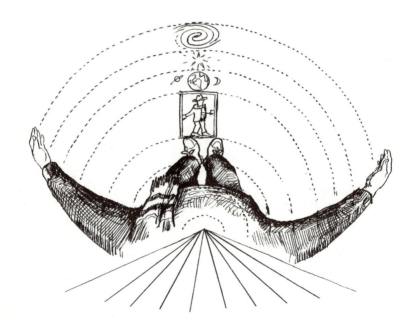

7

Earth's Crammed with Heaven

Earth's crammed with Heaven,
And every common bush afire with God;
But only he who sees takes off his shoes,
The rest sit round it and pluck blackberries,
And daub their natural faces unaware
More and more from the first similitude.
Elizabeth Barrett Browning

Just now, seated on the terrace of this house in the blazing July sunshine, I'm looking at a display of lobelia. To call the blue of the lobelia heavenly is to do it less than justice. It's afire with God. Alight with no "spiritual" fire (whatever that will-o'-the-wisp could mean) but with a more fiery fire, one that surpasses ordinary fire not by being less physical but more physical, by being super-physical. There's a true sense in which Heaven's more substantial, more all-there and embodied than Earth – even more earthy than Earth! – and God more earthy than man. That's why the ways to Him are like that too – precise, active, actual-factual, down-to-Earth, concrete and the opposite of abstract. And moreover thoroughly practical in our everyday dealings with life as it is,

I suppose I could describe my job as ferreting out and sharing and practising ways back to God who is our Home. Which, in ordinary parlance, means that I'm in the spiritual line of business, which you might suppose is other-worldly and unworldly and takes its cue from St. James, who said that true religion and undefiled is "To visit the fatherless and widows in their affliction, and to keep oneself unspotted from the world."

In fact, if we go by this definition of religion I'm as irreligious as they come, this-worldly to the limit and allergic to other-worldliness. In recent months I have been more and more astonished to find just how physical true spirituality is, and just how spiritual true physicality is. How crammed with Heaven Earth is in all sorts of ways. All the approaches that take me to God turn out to be real roads from one real place to an even more real place, traversed by real vehicles that take their time and have their limitations and defects. And – what's still more astonishing – each journey Home is itself an indispensable unfolding of That which is revealed at journey's end. It's what you might call a *REAL-isation which turns idle and nebulous concepts into active and precise percepts*. Or, more briefly, a *Concretisation*. (Yes, I find this repulsive but accurate word in my *Chambers Dictionary*.)

In this chapter I want to take some of the ways Home, and show how what starts off as a commonplace but vague and questionable (if not altogether illusory) notion or appearance ends as a sure and clearly visible and breath-taking Reality. It's not that the spiritual revelation – the Beatific Vision – happens to be compatible with its physical accompaniments and conditions, but that it can't spare them. Heaven's as crammed with Earth as Earth with Heaven. Show me a spiritual something that washes its holy hands of all things common or unclean, and I will show you a mirage, an idle and probably idolatrous dream.

The Door

Please repeat the experiment described in the previous chapter.

Another name for the Hole in the Card is the Door in the Wall – your Door to God. In the Gospel of Thomas we read: "Many stand outside the door, but it's the Alone that goes through to the bride-chamber." Now provided you carried out conscientiously and successfully the two parts of that experiment, you – yes you, out of all the 6,000,000,000 humans now on Earth (to say nothing of all the other sentient beings that are and were and shall be) – are that One. You Alone are clean through that Door into the Alone, as the Alone.

Exactly how did you make sure that you alone are through the Hole or Door? By thinking about it, by working up your feelings, by having faith? Certainly not! You *did* something. You went right up to the Opening and passed through it without the slightest difficulty. And then you looked around and saw that every one of the others was stuck in and blocking the Opening. All the evidence pointed to the awesome fact that, no matter how many myriads happen to be carrying out that experiment along with you, only you are through to the Alone. You relied on your senses to take you to the Alone, and – by God! – they did.

And how can you be sure that it's none other than the Alone that you are through to and united with? Because here and only here you find the Clarity that's perfectly visible because it's perfectly simple, unchanging, boundless, empty, full, and un-moving, *in sharp contrast to all else, to all those more or less invisible and airy-fairy creatures and not-all-there creations.* Again it was your senses that sensed and explored that uniquely divine topography.

Now tell me, what could be more actual-visual-physical than the whole operation? Than your shift from the troublesome side of the wall to the other side, and from your looking at the Divine Clarity to your looking out of it? Than your failure to find any limits to your Spaciousness? Than the collapse of the distance between you and the furthest galaxy? Than your explosion into Immensity?

Archbishop William Temple described Christianity as the most materialistic of the great religions. I think he was right, but however that may be, we can certainly say that this was high praise. If you and I are sure that life aside from our Source is no life at all, if we know that we find ourselves by losing ourselves in Him, and that to refuse the Beatific Vision is to blind ourselves to all true vision, then we will gratefully take the low road, the down-to-earth way Home to Him that He has set up, and will cease playing about with our highfalutin and nebulous and bowdlerised substitutes for it – blind alleys all of them. To despise His Earth is to slam the door on His Heaven.

The Opening of Your Third Eye

They will tell you, of course, that your Third Eye isn't a hard fact but a helpful metaphor, and that there's nothing physical about it, or about its opening or its remaining shut. A metaphor intended in Eastern religions to give some idea of the state of a so-called enlightened soul. And they add that the light in his or her enlightenment is equally metaphorical and unluminous. Similarly here in the West they will tell you that, when Jesus said that "if your eye is single your whole body shall be full of light having no place dark", he wasn't talking about your physical eye but your mental or spiritual state of one-pointedness or attention. And again they will add that the light referred to is a symbol or metaphor or parable indicating a purely spiritual condition. Jesus was keen on parables.

Let's settle the matter right now for good and all, simply by looking to see what happens when you put on your glasses slowly.

The two lenses held in your hands out there come together in one lens here on your nose. You are wearing a monocle. Why are you wearing a monocle? Because you are looking out of One Eye,

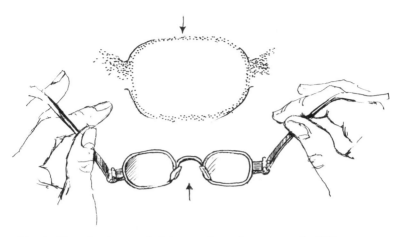

a Single Eye that's much bigger than the monocle. Why are you looking out of a big Single Eye? Because you are Cyclopean.

To find out just how big it is, take off your monocle (thereby turning it into a pair of glasses again) and try to find, with the help of your exploring outstretched arms, the limits of this gigantic Single Eye that you are looking out of.

If you fail to find any limits, if you discover that What you are looking out of is invariably wider than what you are looking at – even when it's sea or sky – how can you claim and take on and account for this world-transcending Eye without taking on its world-transcending Owner? How could you possess and activate so confidently and so smoothly this matchless Organ yet hold aloof from its Operator, from this matchless Cyclopean Organism? (I'm sure He won't mind you calling Him that, in a manner of speaking.)

I leave you to answer these life-and-death questions. My purpose here is to remind you (and of course myself) just how we answer these questions and make these startling and tremendous discoveries about the identity of the One here that sees. We do so by putting on our glasses or sunglasses a little more slowly than usual! You can't get more mundane, more practical and ordinary than that; or arrive anywhere more glorious than the heavenly mansions you are immediately conducted to. Earth doesn't take long to uncram and release Heaven.

As for the light that lights up your Single Eye (they used to call it the Uncreated Light in the Eastern Church), just look and see what it looks like right now. Some Sufis have called it the Light that lights up the light, and St. John's Gospel apostrophises it as the Light that lights every man that comes into the world. I suggest that, of all things in the world, this is just about the most itself and actual-factual, the least symbolic of something else, and none other than the essential light of Heaven.

From Driving Your Land-rover to Driving Your Land

This book is about your potential union with the God of Heaven and Earth; and this chapter is about the very earthly demonstrations and proofs and practices which will (if you allow them) assure you of that very heavenly unification; and this section is about the most earth-shaking of those demonstrations and proofs and practices. Literally earth-shaking, world-moving, a spectacular upheaval if ever there was one.

How shall you know for sure that you are united to Him? By consulting your feelings? They will tell you many contradictory and confusing stories. By stricter discipline and keeping yourself unspotted from the world? That could take you further than ever from its Creator. By theologising, and seeking to understand, for instance, what Aristotle meant when he described God as the Unmoved Mover of the world. What a hope! Are you sure he understood it?

You have to come off your sophisticated mental-spiritual pedestal, come down to earth and be honest and simple enough to look at and take seriously what's going on. Humble enough, for instance, to notice the strange behaviour of the lamp-posts hurrying past your car.

Everybody, of course, will tell you that it's not the lamp-posts but you and your car that are hurrying along at 60mph. And that the whole of the scenery from hedges to hills and mountain-tops stays quite still, and any movements it seems to have are, of course, altogether illusory. Of course.

Now I put it to you that God's telling you one thing about lamp-posts and Man's telling you a very different thing, and that it's up to you make your choice. A very great deal hangs on that choice. It's like this: God's inviting you to station yourself in the central Immobility from which He moves all things including lamp-posts, to share fully in this vivid demonstration of His power and His glory. What's more, He goes to astonishing lengths to press this superb gift on you. Whereas Man says to you: "Go by what I tell you, not by what you see, and you will be one of Us, a Club Member. Obey the Club's rules, or else", God says to you "I'm not asking you to have faith and believe that you and I are One, but to go by the evidence. I'm doing all I can to show you."

Further, it seems to me that the sensible way of choosing between these alternatives is to look and see What you are Where you are When you are driving your car (as they say). I think you will see something like this –

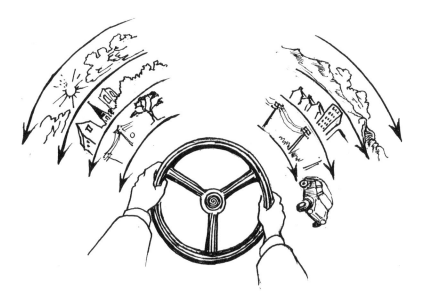

It is characteristic of *things* that they move. Those hands of yours on the steering wheel and those feet on the pedals are certainly things which move. But the You that's nearer to you than those mobile limbs, busy putting them forth, the You that (on present evidence) You are looking out of – is manifestly No-thing, and it's impossible to budge an Absence-of-anything-to-budge. So much for You, now for your world. Please shift your attention to the road ahead. I'm confident that you will find it's a kind of winding, widening, fast-flowing asphalt river on which you are securely moored. As for the landscape in all its details far and near, *that*, and not your Land-Rover, is what you are manifestly driving!

Really I can't see how His invitation to participate in His Divine Nature, with all the Power and the Glory of it, could be couched in stronger or more pressing or persuasive terms. Or how thoroughly and vividly, down to the last physical detail, His Earth could be packed any more full of His Heaven than it is. The No-thing that is Every-thing is that generous!

No Matter How

No matter how vociferously I declare that I'm based on and living from the human being that you see, I'm really based on and living from the Divine Being that you don't see, that I really am at Centre. I have to Be Right Here about Myself before I can be wrong there about myself!

No matter how negative my feelings about you and how bad my behaviour, the fact is that I give my life, my very being, for you. How could I possibly take you on without taking myself off, or see you without unseeing me? How can I undermine those negative feelings and that bad behaviour more radically than by seeing they have no real foundation?

No matter how distant I believe the stars are, and all those other objects near and far, the only way I can be in receipt of them is to abolish their distance, to coincide with them. I must have them here before I can dispatch them to what I call their proper places.

No matter how convinced I am that I'm binocular, I was never and will never be anything but monocular. I'm living from and seeing out of the way I am, into the way I'm not. I can't hallucinate peripherally without ceasing to do so centrally.

No matter how small I think I am, how can I not explode in all directions to infinity?

No matter how old I think I am, how can I age where there's nothing to age?

No matter how sick I am, my medicine is nearer to me than my sickness and more potent.

No matter how bad I am at being this and that and the other, I couldn't be better at Being – and Not-Being.

Let's sum up our findings in this chapter. The Flower is beautiful but always brief and often blighted. However tasty, the Fruit rots and is frequently as bitter as wormwood. But the Root is nurturing and perennial and absolutely sound. "The world is charged with the grandeur of God," and there really does live "the dearest freshness deep down things." Turn on the telly or read the news and take your daily dose of Hell, top it up with a list of all the things that are going wrong in your own life, then tell me what grounds for hope remain. Surely an optimist is either a fraud or a fool, you reply. Not necessarily. He could be you who, greatly daring, at long last go much more by what you see than by what you are taught and told to see, or are tricked into pretending you see. You who are ceasing to suppress the fact that Earth is Earth solely because she's sitting comfortably on Heaven's lap. You who see ever more clearly how God's happy and fascinating truths about you expose and get the better of all those terribly unhappy and tedious social fictions.

8

Miss Chipperfield and the Water-colourist of the World

Funny things happen in our childhood, curious indications of our real character, of our mission or destiny, which seem to set the course of our whole life. Or at least to point out the direction it's likely to take. At the time, of course, they aren't seen as at all prophetic. It's only in retrospect that we tumble to the far-reaching significance of these early happenings. So it comes about that our life, though lived forwards, is understood backwards, and the child is revealed as indeed 'the father of the man', as Wordsworth put it.

Hindsight tells me that Wordsworth was right, at least so far as this child is concerned. Not only did I get off to an unusually early start with my life's work, but I began with some of the best of it.

I was about six years old at the time. Our house stood on top of a cliff overlooking the slate-coloured North Sea, and the sea-weedy wreck of a fishing vessel called The Spider. I was in the habit of wandering along the windy and desolate shore, alone. And it was here that I discovered my mine of jewels - rubies, emeralds, turquoises, amethysts, topazes, what have you. Mind you, they were a gradual discovery and took a lot of patient unearthing. Some of the more beautiful ones - for instance the rubies - were rare and proportionately precious. But I was a frequent and hard-working miner. And how richly my efforts were rewarded!

For these weren't the ordinary sort of precious stones you find in jewellers' shop windows, the sort that are set in rings and necklaces and crowns. Oh no! Those were mere jewels, fairly common and quite unmagical: bright and beautiful like my own gems, of course, but ordinary, not at all mysterious, and quite powerless.

Mine, on the other hand, were altogether special. In fact, unique, and so different that they deserved other names. To call them super-rubies or super-emeralds and so on, or even the real Crown Jewels, didn't begin to do justice to the magical potency of my treasures. Or perhaps I should say: to the worldwide magic power they conferred upon their delighted owner – conferred upon me, this seemingly commonplace and much-put-upon small boy.

This magical power was the ability to paint the world all over, from the highest fleecy cloud in the sky to my own hand, from the tiny steamer on the horizon to the foaming breakwater at my feet, instantly, whatever the colour of my choice. And then, instantly, to change that colour from (say) red to blue, and then from blue to amber, as the mood took me. And not only was this magic quite secret (I was careful not to tell even my best friends about it), but it was evidently one that all others lacked absolutely. No matter what they held to their eye, what gem they chose to look through, nothing happened to the scene. It stayed the same old colour. Only I had the right to call myself the water-colourist of the world!

Of course the language I use now to describe my childhood experience is very different from what I would have used then. In fact I had neither the ability nor the need to spell out these things in any detail. And surely they were all the more thrilling, more deeply felt, on that account.

No wonder, then, that the upshot, the tragic conclusion of my gem-mining adventure, was so devastating. So much so that I remember the scene to this day, vividly and in detail – the echoing schoolroom and the view from its window of my deserted beach and the angry sea.

The ogre of the occasion was Miss Chipperfield, the iron-monger's elderly daughter. She was one of the teachers – the only nasty one – in Miss Smith's dame-school, which I attended daily. She noticed – she would! – that the pockets of my off-white shorts bulged suspiciously, and made me turn them out. And then she had the nerve, the wickedness, to call my precious jewels dirty rubbish, bits of filthy broken glass which were already spoiling my shorts and would be sure to cut me before long.

Well, I cried and cried. I begged to keep at least my rubies. But in vain. Into the iron rubbish bin they all went, and were lost for ever. And what was even worse, my parents were told, and further mining was strictly prohibited. How I cursed Miss Chipperfield! From then on I made sure she taught me nothing.

Not that the wretched woman was able to strip me of all my magic powers, however much she would have liked to. There was another power that came to me even earlier than world-colour-ing. I gave it no name at the time, but *world-owning* will do. Though less spectacular than *world-colouring*, it did have the advantage that nobody could guess what I was up to, much less put a stop to it.

In those far-off days young children were got out of the way by sending them to bed at seven o'clock, or even earlier. The window of my bedroom had, instead of a curtain, a shiny buff roller-blind, covered with brown arabesques, which let in most of the light on a summer evening, and, in winter, most of the glare of the street arc-lamps. So it was that, unable to get to sleep and forbidden to get up, I lay there for hours contemplating those brown arabesques. Utterly boring though they were in them-selves, I found I could, by steady staring, do a marvellous thing with them. I could bring them right up to me! And, after some practice, other things, too, no matter how distant they were said to be. Now the charm of this magic wasn't only that, in spite of its worldwide operation, it remained perfectly secret, but also that the collapse of their distance made things mine. When thus truly seen, all I laid eyes on became my very own property. But again, of course, I didn't indulge in any such word-play. It was enough that somehow I lived my everywhereness and allness. It made a lot of difference. For instance, when the streetlights went out and I raised the blind a little, I could see the stars into my bedroom. Or was it that I could see myself into their bedroom? Either way, there's magic for you!

There are two other kinds of equally impressive world-magic that I must touch on here, more briefly because they are fairly well known. As well-known as they are undervalued.

The first we call *world-destroying-and-world-re-creating*. Or, if you want to rubbish it, *the ostrich ploy*. One buries one's head in the bedclothes, thereby suddenly abolishing the Universe down to the last bit of fluff. And then, after a suitable interval devoted to relishing one's mighty destructive power, suddenly produces everything out of nothing, arrayed in all its former splendour and why-there-it-isness!

The second we call *world-turning*. When I start rotating on the spot – wow! – I do nothing of the kind. I start everything else rotating, and the nearer it is the faster it goes. The whole scene whirling like mad, around what? Why around its true Centre, of course.

Add this expertise to world-colouring, world-owning, world-destroying, and world-re-creating, and you have something big! An impressive magic repertoire, far surpassing all adult cleverness, and quite encouraging for a child who's always being reminded by grown-ups that he's not grown up.

Most of us soon grow out of this sort of thing. I have grown into it. That world-shrinking adventure in the lonesome bedroom and that world-painting adventure on the draughty foreshore, were early steps along the road I had to go, a powerful kick-start to the whole thrust and purpose of my life. So far from chipperfielding those childhood powers, I have made it my business to take them very seriously indeed.

Why? For a variety of good reasons. Because they were and are based on what I see instead of what I'm told I see. Because they can be verified by anyone anywhere at any time. Because they dovetail neatly into that perennial philosophy which I find makes intellectual and practical sense of an otherwise chaotic and meaningless existence. Because I cannot believe they were awarded to me by an Almighty Trickster hell-bent on fooling me. And (may I add for good measure?) because they are so intriguing, such good fun, so productive of further magic; and as such more than enough to keep me busy all these years.

Wordsworth got it right. We do come trailing clouds of glory from God who is our Home. But in a deeper sense we never left Home. Nor need the glory dim with age, much less depart forever. It can still blaze out of bits of filthy broken glass in rubbish dumps by angry seas. It still can and it still does tickle into leaping back and forth lazy old arabesques on shiny roller blinds. The glory can and should flood our whole life. Shades of the prison-house don't have to close in forever around the growing and grown-up boy or girl. Anyone of any age, who really wants to, can see his or her way out of jail into the happy and inexhaustible astonishments of freedom.

The author of this book is a nonagenarian child who suffered some very severe attacks of adulthood, but has largely recovered. Witness the fact that when he finds himself redecorating the land-scape and skyscape, or making or unmaking or spinning it all, he's just as bowled over as when he did those same things at the age of six. And more determined than ever that all the Chipperfields in all the world, aided and abetted by that little old grown-up in his mirror, shall not prevent him.

'Truly I say to you: whosoever will not receive the Kingdom of Heaven as a little child will not enter it.'

9

VISIOTHERAPY

The nine grades of beings are all in your physical body.
The illuminated man liberates his inner living beings,
even before they take shape in him.
Zen Master Hui Hai

Hui Hai, affectionately known as The Great Pearl, was a famous Zen master of the T'ang Dynasty. But though he lived more than a thousand years ago, and was as Chinese as they come, he raises questions that we modern Westerners - shame on us! - have hardly thought of asking. Questions of huge prophylactic importance, even of life and death. What's more, I think we shall find him pointing a steady forefinger at their answer.

Taking our cue from Hui Hai, we shall in this chapter be addressing such questions as these. How therapeutic is Self-realisation? Is the discovery of our true Nature good for us physically as well as mentally and spiritually, or does it make very little difference? Do our "interior living beings" (our cells for example, as we would say) somehow share in our Self-realisation anyway? Or is there something we can do to help along that sharing? If so, what? In their liberated or illuminated state (whatever that could mean) are they more likely to do a good job, and less likely to give us trouble? Less likely, for example, to split into warring factions and "selfishly" multiply here and there at the expense of the body as a whole, as in cancer?

We shall try, of course, to reach definite conclusions that can at once be put into practice. Where we fail, we shall perhaps be able to suggest some promising lines of research to the experts – that is, to seers who are also physicians or therapists of one sort or another. Is there a place (we shall be asking them) for what I call Visiotherapy in their professional practice, in medicine generally, in prophylaxis? Should the Self-realised healer himself prescribe, and maybe in suitable cases himself administer, a course of Eye-opening exercises? Is decapitation or cephalotomy (amputating the wen-like growth on the shoulders of the First Person) worthy of inclusion in the healing arts? After all, if it's agreed that such remedies heal the mind and the spirit, it wouldn't be surprising if the body followed suit in ways yet to be discovered. Taking on, perhaps, not just a temporary and superficial tone or glow, or releasing unforeseen energies for dealing with unforeseen crises, but also drawing on a profounder, more secret, more sustained Resource, to which every level of one's being has access.

At this point it's worth noticing how, in the hyperbolical manner of the Mahayana, Hui Hai describes the physical conse-quences of 'liberating one's interior beings'. Among the thirty-two bodily (*bodily!*) marks of Buddhahood that the seer displays (he says) are a golden complexion and a universe-penetrating radiance. And all the while, underpinning this splendour, is the Void in which the seer is consciously rooted, the Emptiness that performs 'innumerable functions which respond unfailingly to circumstances'. One is reminded of Moses's shining face when he came down from the mountain, of the transfigur-ation of Jesus on that other mountain, and of those saints whose interior illumin-ation shone through for all to see. After all allow-ances have been made for pious rhetoric and hagiographical exaggeration, there remains plenty of evidence that spiritual and physical well-being do often go together. At the very least, then, let us take these traditional stories as a picturesque confirmation that here's a field whose exploration is urgent.

For a start, let's note how far we can get with what's beyond all reasonable doubt. I'm referring to the fact that our central Emptiness (call it what we will – Void, Clarity, Spirit, Awake Capacity, Conscious No-thingness, or simply What's-now-taking-in-this-printing) is stripped of all traces and kinds of ownership, wiped clean of every personal label and distinguishing mark and indication of grade or status. It belongs to and is equally at home on all hierarchical levels. Manifestly What sees Itself here as Clarity is neither my Clarity, nor your Clarity, nor his or her Clarity, nor its Clarity, but *the* Clarity, indivisible, universal. As indicated on our sketch-map of the First Person Singular, it's the Central Non-Being that lies at the Core of the countless beings it's forever giving rise to.

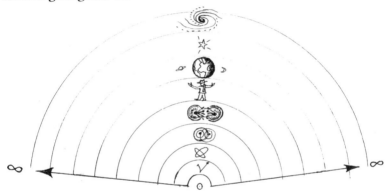

In other words, when you see into the Reality at your Centre, into What those countless regional appearances of yours are appearances of, you do so as none other than that all-embracing Reality itself. You do so as me and for me, and as and for everyone else as well. In fact your enlightenment is no different from and none other than the Buddha's, which – according to an ancient tradition – necessarily involved the enlightenment of all sentient beings of every grade and era. It's a tradition that's way ahead of our time, and one that sounds a timely warning. Though 'my' enlightenment is so obviously not mine, (no truly enlightened being sees itself surrounded by endarkened beings) my 'ego' says it is mine. Therefore let me tread cautiously as I venture into the field of enlightenment. Let me never forget that it's a minefield in both senses, and vigilance is essential if I'm not to be blown ego-sky-high.

The Clarity that I find here, that I am at Centre, is the inside story and root aspect of my 'interior beings' of every grade. It's cellular no less than human, for instance. I need to take this fact very seriously, take it to heart. It won't do to look down occasionally from above and casually acknowledge my debt to and oneness at Centre with these humble servitors. I began this life some ninety-three years ago as just one of them (as an almost invisible egg) and still am that original cell *en famille*, so to say. To ignore or deny these humbling home truths (and who of us doesn't do just that?) is risky. It's as if one's cells hate being overlooked and despised, and make their annoyance felt. What happens at the social level when the rulers get out of touch with the ruled should warn us of the consequences of similar insensitivity at the human-cellular level. The Servile Wars of Ancient Rome, the Peasants' Revolt in medieval England, the Jacquerie and the French Revolution, with all their horrors, happened because the upper classes were too class-ridden, too uppish, to put themselves in the shoes of the lower classes, to feel for them and act accordingly. No wonder the common folk rebelled. By the same token, would it be surprising if my cell-population – despised as immeasurably inferior by the upstart boss who began life as one of them, if not ignored altogether – should rebel? And conversely, would it be surprising if, when I consciously become one at Centre with each and all of them, that they and I should together enjoy better health and a lot more vitality?

I can hear you raising a couple of objections at this point. The first runs like this. Ramana Maharshi, who we agree was a great sage and seer, died of cancer, as did Nisargadatta and other highly gifted spiritual masters. Am I saying that their enlightenment was in some way deficient, not deep enough?

To which I reply: Ramana was indeed a profoundly self-realised soul. And he was also an Indian ascetic who in his youth chose to live in a dark and noisome vault beneath a temple. His biographer Arthur Osborne writes: 'It was seldom that any human being entered; only ants, vermin and mosquitoes flourished there. They preyed on him till his thighs were covered with sores that ran pus and blood. To the end of his life the marks remained.' Nor was he indifferent to his body and its welfare. He described the body as 'a disease'. His interior beings took their revenge, sage though he was.

The second objection isn't so much a No as a Yes-but. Here's how it goes. Granted that consciously sharing your enlightenment with your cells may well be good for them and you, and may make cancer somewhat less likely, it's only one of numerous factors, and perhaps only a minor one, at that. The immense research effort that's being put into the kinds and causes and treatment of cancer has so far come up with no overriding, clear, and simple answers. Heredity, smoking, junk food, pollution, stress, artificial lifestyles in general – these are some of the aetiological factors under investigation, to which may well be added a negative or hostile attitude to your interior beings of any grade and all grades. But to make exaggerated or over-confident claims for Visiotherapy would be no use at all in the fight against this and other degenerative diseases.

So much for our second objection.

All this I readily admit and indeed insist on – so far as it goes. Which isn't nearly far enough. There's another and very different side to my embodiment. Truly I have two bodies. As a second-third person I have a small, dying, disease-prone body, while as a first person (or rather as *the* First Person Singular) I have a Resurrection Body which in all important respects is the opposite of the body that my doctor looks after and I find in

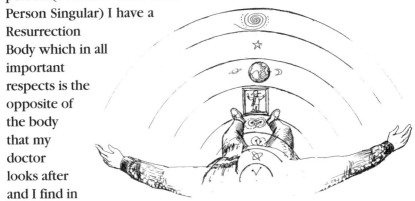

my mirror. Now instead of laboriously cataloguing the differences between these two bodies, let me sum them up in a picture.

The questions I put to myself are these. When I clearly see and take on and get used to my Resurrection Body, when I enjoy and live in the light of What I really am region by region, as distinct from what I look like to you, what are the regional effects? When I consciously travel from my human region a metre or so away, through my cellular region, and my molecular and atomic and subatomic regions, to this absolutely deserted Centre, are the inhabitants of those hierarchical regions refreshed or in any way affected? Up to now I have found that in all-important respects my pseudo-life in that second-third-person body contrasts sharply with my real life in this First-Person-Body. Now I think it would be strange if this contrast ceased when it came to the question of health and ill-health. Very strange indeed if 'my' enlightenment, which (as we have seen is in fact all-level) were to manifest and take full effect only at the human level. Surely it's up to me to endorse and not obstruct that full effect at all levels.

Visiotherapy is therapy in depth or not therapy at all. How does it work? To take a particular instance, how does its deep treatment of cancer compare with chemotherapy and radiotherapy?

Chemotherapy and radiotherapy aim to kill off as many diseased cells as possible, and as few healthy cells as possible.

Visiotherapy works along similar lines but is much more drastic. It succeeds in killing them all off and starting all over again. In Christian terms, it is that Death and Rebirth which is the price of entry into the Kingdom of Heaven. In fact, as indicated on our sketch-map, it takes the form of a real journey through real space to the No-thing that's the common Core of all things. To the absolutely disease-free

No-thing that, with the aid of this in-pointing finger, I discover right here, busy exploding into Every-thing. In other words, into this single-eyed and wide-armed and all-level Resurrection Body of mine.

This alone is my real Body, my strictly indivisible cosmic constitution, of which my human body is a minute and temporary fragment. Without my fellow humans I'm not human, and without my fellow organisms I'm not alive. What am I, again, without my molecular and atomic and subatomic ingredients? Or without my Earth and Sun and Galaxy? The truth is that the whole of me is nothing less than the Whole, the entire cosmic hierarchy ranging from the all-inclusive One to the all-exclusive None. As complete, as First-person, I'm not in the world – the world's in me – and all beings are my interior beings. In sober truth, just as my Body is indivisible, so its health is indivisible. And Visiotherapy is practising the shift from one's pseudo-body, through one's no-body, to one's true and total Body. Which is always in good nick.

So much for my amateurish outline of the case for Visiotherapy. Over to the professionals, to you physicians and therapists who are also seers of your true Identity. Here an arduous and long-term research programme awaits you, one which promises to be as fascinating as it is needful.

In conclusion, back to Hui Hai. I think he well deserves the title of The Great Pearl, if only for teaching that the liberated man liberates his interior beings even before they take shape in him. And when he tells me that the nine grades of being are all in my physical body he surely speaks the truth. A millennium ahead of his time, he even gets the number right, bless him! Reading from galaxies to particles, I count nine, too!

Salutations to the Master!

10

I LIVE, YET NOT I

I am crucified with Christ,
nevertheless I live:
yet not I,
but Christ lives in me.
St Paul

Scattered thinly throughout the past two millennia there have been Christians – I'm tempted to call them real Christians – for whom these words of St Paul are literally true and by no means figurative or metaphorical. These are men and women who take this tremendous but puzzling assertion of his seriously, who apply it to themselves personally and practise what amounts to a funda-mental identity-shift from a merely human identity to one that's primarily divine. Gifted and trusting souls who can say with Paul 'It pleased God, who separated me from my mother's womb, to reveal His Son in me.' Fortunate ones, blessed with great faith, who go on to prove in everyday life the reality of what they had assumed to be true.

I am a man of little faith, a Doubting Thomas who feels like saying to Paul: 'Though I long to discover that Christ the God-Man is in me as my life, that He is much more *me* than the very unChristlike fellow pictured in my passport and my mirror is *me*, I just can't believe it.' The proposition is far too wild and far too flattering to take on trust. For what it amounts to is the claim that I, who have every reason to regard myself as a momentary and infinitesimal and far-from-admirable fragment of the world, am in fact pregnant with (or even in some sense identical with) its infinite and ineffable Origin. To believe that story because I was told to believe it, or because I would like to believe it, seems to me pitiful and ridiculous, and certainly no compliment to that Origin.

So I say to Paul, 'Show me. Telling me is no use. I'll believe in the Christ who is my life when I see and feel Him living my life, when He's so blazingly obvious right here that I can no longer doubt His presence and my shift of identity onto Him.'

But I go too fast. First I must be clear Who Christ is for me, what I mean by that exalted but heavily loaded and ambiguous title. Let me then list what I take to be His essential attributes, the characteristics I would have to take on if – wonder of all impossible wonders! – I were to switch from being Douglas Edison Harding to being Him and living His life, Paul-fashion or any fashion whatever.

Well, here's my list. It's not precisely yours, I guess, or what a priest or a theologian would come up with, but near enough for our purpose.

1   Self-giving

The very nature of Christ is self-giving love, to the point of dying so that you and I may live.

2   Crucifixion

One of the things that makes His death so special is the manner of it. He's the Crucified One.

3   A New Body

Now risen from the dead, however, He takes on a drastically remodelled resurrection body, hard for those of us who are on this side of Death to imagine.

4   Omnipresence

But He's certainly not imprisoned or exclusively located in His resurrection body. He's everywhere, at large, all the while.

5   Imperishability

Like all of Space, all of Time is in Him, the Eternal One.

6   Centrality

Not only does He pervade Space and Time, but all of it proceeds from Him and returns to Him who lies at its unique Centre.

7   Inclusiveness

Everything and everyone, no matter how remote or how defective, how miserable or how sinful, is embraced by Him, is held in His great heart.

8   Purity

Yet He remains uncontaminated, serene, spotless, in every way perfect.

9   Stillness

His perfection includes perfect tranquillity and peace and rest, and it's from His immobility that all things are moved.

10   Omnipotence

In fact, He's all-powerful, inasmuch as in the last resort His will is done.

11   Omniscience

And as all-wise He has perfect insight into what all beings really are. He knows them so much better that they know themselves.

12   God into Man, Man into God

And yet, notwithstanding this galaxy of transcendent attributes, He is Man as well as God, human no less than divine.

Well, that's my First List. It describes what I'm not like, but would have to be like if Christ lived in me and were my life. To put it another way, here are no fewer than twelve powerful reasons why I'm not Him, a round dozen respects in which, quite obviously, I fall immeasurably short of His divine perfection. All these, with more lurking for sure, whereas just one of them would have been enough to bar me forever from Christhood!

How right I was to refuse point-blank to *believe* the Apostle, and demand to be *shown* that Christ is - or one day could become - my life and my very being. So what I propose to do now is to take a fresh look at myself, just in case I can catch a glimpse of what Paul was talking about, and of some way to bridge the huge gap between me and the Christ that lived in him. With this end in view, let me make my Second List.

It's not, this time, a list of the attributes of Christ as I conceive Him to be out there, but of myself as I perceive myself to be right here. And by *myself* I do not mean the fellow I see over there in my mirror, but the very different fellow I see this side of the glass, the one who does the seeing. For purposes of comparison I combine the two lists - Christ's attributes in italics, my own in ordinary print. At least this juxtaposition should help to highlight the contrast between Him and me.

I think that this rough map, for checking against what's on show, will prove as useful to you throughout as it does to me.

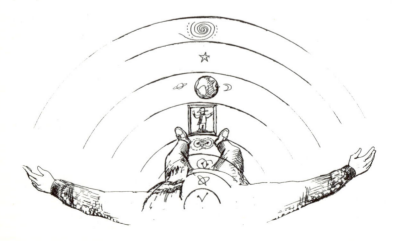

Because of course I'm not asking you to believe anything, but to discover at every stage whether you happen to find yourself to be pretty much what I find myself to be.

1 Self-giving

The very nature of Christ is self-giving love, to the point of dying so that you and I may live.

Right here, at the mid-point of the map, I perceive myself to be Empty Space, Capacity, Room for whatever's presenting itself. If it's you that's turning up here, I have nothing to keep you out with, and I vanish in your favour. If there remained so much as a dustgrain it would be enough to crowd you out absolutely. But nothing's left. I see nothing my side of you. The price of your appearance here, in all its wonderful richness and givenness, is my poverty and not-givenness, my disappearance. The truth is that I give my life and very being for you, not because I'm self-denying or saintly (very far from it!) but because I have no option.

2 Crucifixion

One of the things that make His death so special is the manner of it. He's the Crucified One.

Looking straight ahead and raising my arms to shoulder height, I gradually spread them till they almost vanish. And I see, with some astonishment, that these huge arms of mine – in total contrast to those of other people – embrace the wide world, the whole of what's on show. My left hand is further from my right hand than sunrise from sunset, than East from West. And it's not only that this all-inclusive gesture is cruciform. I find myself participating in the suffering that goes with crucifixion.

3 A New Body

Now risen from the dead, however, He takes on a drastically re-modelled, resurrection body, hard for us who are on this side of Death to imagine.

Looking here to see the actually-given shape of my body, I find that it's different from all the bodies around me (including the one in my mirror) in at least four striking respects. (a) Mounted on their shoulders is just one head apiece, whereas mounted on mine is accommodation for all the heads I come across. The fact is that I'm beheaded (and there's no death more certain and summary than beheading) and already living a many-headed resurrection life. (b) As if to make up for being a little shorter than my companions, I'm immeasurably wider, as we have already seen. (c) Also I'm the reverse of the others: the other way up and facing the other way. And (d) I'm furnished with a Single Eye that's even wider than the world it's taking in, whereas they sport a pair of peep-holes in a small bone box. And of course there are many other instances of the difference between me and them: for example, the fact that my hands are normally so much bigger than my feet. But I guess I've said enough to show how great is the contrast between this postmortem body and those pre-mortem bodies.

4   Omnipresence

But He's certainly not imprisoned or exclusively located in His resurrection body. He's everywhere, at large, all the while.

Right here is What's holding out these two huge arms of mine, which is also What I'm looking out of. Pointing in now at this wide-awake What, I find No-thing at all, an Emptiness which has exploded to infinity. The centre of the cosmic circle has devoured all its radii. Thus I perceive no distance between me and the thing I'm looking at. And a ruler held up between my Eye and your eye, being end-on, reduces to zero. By the same token the 'furthest' galaxy or star or planet is nearer than near, and all I see I see here. In a word, I'm omnipresent.

5   Imperishability

Like all of Space, all of Time is in Him, the Eternal One.

As the aware No-thing that contains all these changing and perishing things, I'm changeless, timeless, without beginning or end. If I should doubt this I have only to consult my watch. Normally it tells me the time over there. But when I bring it up to my Eye it tells me the no-time right here. And, suffering the fate of all things, itself perishes in the telling.

6   Centrality

Not only does He pervade the Cosmos, but all of it proceeds from and returns to Him who is the unique Centre of everything.

I take up the ruler again and with it prolong downwards the vertical lines around me – such as the corners of the room and the door-jambs – and discover that they all converge upon and radiate from me! From the region of my heart, to be precise. As a child I was told that parallel lines meet at infinity, and now I see that I am that Infinity. What's more, it's Infinity self-aware. Here and nowhere else do I find the Awareness that brings everything to being and life and meaning. If I seem to find it elsewhere that's only because I brought it with me.

7   Inclusiveness

And everything and everyone, no matter how remote or defective, how miserable or sinful, is embraced by Him, is held in His great Heart.

This immense and self-aware emptiness that I find here isn't just empty. It's empty-for-filling. Ultimately no-one and nothing is left out. In fact I'm not well, not quite sane, not 'all there', not whole till I'm the Whole. Nor, to put it another way, is the Universe whole while I split it into an observer here and an observed there, into a me-part and a not-me-part. To enjoy the Universe as a *Uni*verse, and no longer to suffer from it as a *Duo*verse, I have to be none of it centrally and all of it peripherally. They are two sides of the coin.

8   Purity

Yet He remains absolutely uncontaminated, serene, spotless, in every way perfect.

Looking up from what I'm writing, I point in two directions at once. With my right forefinger in at What's looking. And with my left forefinger out at what's being looked at – namely a settee, some chairs, a window. And I notice three things. First, how total is the contrast between the emptiness here and what's filling it there. Second, how total, nevertheless, is their unity. Third, how uncontaminated the emptiness is by its filling. For when I turn to view another part of the room, I take none of the previous part (settee, chairs, window) with me. The emptiness that I am stays clean, empty for each new scene, forever virginal, immaculate.

9   Stillness

His perfection includes perfect tranquillity and peace and rest, yet it is from His immobility that all things are moved,

While I can find excuses for overlooking the obvious fact that post-mortem I'm stainless, I can find none for overlooking the even more obvious fact that post-mortem I'm motionless. In the train, at the wheel of my car, or simply going for a walk, I have only to see what I see instead of what I'm told to see. Coming to my senses, I stop denying that everything from distant hills to wayside telegraph poles is the move in me, who am the all-enveloping Stillness, the Unmoved Mover of the world.

10   Omnipotence

In fact, He's all-powerful, inasmuch as His will is done in the long run.

I find in me two wills, one that belongs to the pre-mortem life of the one in my mirror, and the other which belongs to the post-mortem life of the one this side of my mirror. The former is quick to say NO! to a good half of what happens to me, while the latter eventually says YES! – SO BE IT! – to it all. And does so with good reason: I see that right here all my resistance is dissolved and I'm burst wide open to receive whatever's in store for me. Saying Yes! to it is often excruciatingly difficult, of course, but it turns out to be the recipe for the only peace worth having. And so at last the paradox holds: it's because I have no will that my will is done. Right here, total impotence and total omnipotence come to the same thing,

11   Omniscience

And as all-wise He has perfect access to what all beings really are: He knows them so much better than they know themselves.

Clearly seeing into 'my' true and boundless and eternal Nature right here at Centre, I clearly see into 'yours' whoever and whatever and whenever you are, for right here you and I are the same thing – or rather, no-thing. That other kind of omniscience which includes monitoring the behaviour of every particle in the Universe is an idle dream, and a hideous nightmare at that.

12 God into Man, Man into God

And yet, notwithstanding this galaxy of transcendent attributes, He is Man as well as God, human no less than divine.

What is the status of the one whose portrait I have just painted – my status? There's much about it that's human – the shape of these arms, for instance, and the aches and pains in them, and their constant replacement – but also much that's superhuman – their dimensions, for instance, and their all-inclusiveness. Here, in toto, is a breath-taking but wonderfully serviceable apotheosis. Is there any other sort that's readily verifiable and makes sense? Right here, held up for my most searching inspection, is the real and ever-ready answer to all those volumes of convoluted and often bitter (and occasionally lethal) controversy about the Man who is God and the God who is Man, and how the two natures can merge yet remain distinct. But what's much more important is that here is my blueprint for living, all day and every day, the resurrection life, a life that's truly human at last because it's truly divine, and vice versa. A centred life.

Well, there they are, all twelve of Christ's attributes as I conceive them, set against my own corresponding attributes as I perceive them. My central and post-mortem attributes (I hasten to remind you) in stark contrast to the pre-mortem attributes of the fellow called Harding, who is off-Centre by a metre or so, and quite another kettle of fish.

I don't know about you, but I can't get over my amazement at how close the fit is.

I hope you found the map useful. I certainly did, and do. I drew what I saw and was informed and fascinated. Then I saw what I drew, and was devastated! I pray God I will never recover from the shock of that happy vision. The only thing that really matters to me, as I near the end of that off-Centre pre-mortem life, is union with my timeless Source, my identity-shift to the One who is at the same time altogether other than me and more me than I am myself. And I find that this map of the shift helps that shift along wonderfully. Also that it rounds off the familiar icon of the Crucified Saviour giving His life for me long ago and far away, with this unfamiliar icon of the Risen Saviour living His life right here and right now in me. Just as Paul said.

Let's listen to Paul again, while noticing how our map helps us to understand him. 'There is one glory of the sun, and another glory of the moon, and another glory of the stars: for one star differs from another star in glory. So also is the resurrection from the dead. It is sown in corruption and raised in incorruption. It is sown in dishonour, it is raised in glory. It is sown in weakness, it is raised in power. It is sown a natural body, it is raised a spiritual body.'

Finally and for good measure, here are a few more variations on our theme, on what George Herbert called his 'onely musick'.

St Symeon the New Theologian We awaken in Christ's body as He awakens in our body, and my poor hand is Christ. He enters my foot, and is infinitely me. I move my hand and wonderfully it is Christ.

Meister Eckhart What matters is that Christ's birth should happen in me. Discover this birth in you, and you shall discover all good and all comfort, all happiness, all being and all truth… God shines in with His Light and brings in with Him all you forsook and a thousand times more, together with a new form to contain it all.

Henry Suso He (Suso) asked one of the bright Princes of Heaven what God's hidden dwelling-place in the soul looked like… Then he looked in and saw that his body above his heart was as clear as crystal… The blessed are stripped of their personal initiative and changed into another form, another glory, another power.

Jan van Ruysbroeck God the Heavenly Father created all men in His image and His likeness. His image is His Son, His own Eternal Wisdom, and St John says that in this all things have life.

George Herbert Christ is my onely head, my onely heart and breast, my onely musick.

Gerard Manley Hopkins I am at once what Christ is, since He was what I am, and this Jack, joke, poor potsherd, patch, matchwood, is immortal diamond.

11

IMAGINATION
HAS A
WHITE TAIL

Here's a true story.

I mentioned to my parents, one day, that I had just seen a rabbit walking down the High Street of our town.

"Imagination!" they said.

"Does imagination have a white tail?" I asked, in all innocence. I was, you see, about four years old at the time.

The sequel, which is another true story, happened eighty-eight years later.

I said: "I've just seen a wiggle-waggle walking down the High Street."

"Imagination!" they said.

"Does imagination walk upside-down," I asked them, "and make the High Street walk down him, and spread his arms as wide as the world, and wear a topless white waistcoat, like this?

12

THE FALL OF MAN

Along with its counterpart the Salvation of Man, the Fall of Man is one of those religious dogmas that we can do very well without nowadays. Anyone who goes round buttonholing strangers and demanding to know if they are saved is asking for trouble.

Nevertheless the Fall is a fact. Not only is it a psychological come-down, but also a physical descent through physical space from top to bottom. It's just as if every one of us, early in his or her life, tumbles into a very deep well, and is in grave danger of staying trapped down there for the rest of that life.

Obviously, when anyone falls into a well, the good space that stretched harmlessly or usefully beneath him, underfoot, suddenly becomes the bad space that stretches above him, overhead, cutting him off from his world. He's hurt, lonely, famished, and doomed to die an early death - unless some friend hears his cries and hauls him to safety and the blessed sunlight.

What happens, of course, if by great good fortune he is saved, is that his fall is gone through in reverse. The space that stretched so cruelly above his head in the well is thrust beneath his feet again and rendered innocuous.

I'll now re-tell this three-part story as I figure it has worked out in my own life. The early details are speculative, but I'll vouch for the overall picture.

Before the Fall

When I first saw the stars they were dear little things I could tickle without pricking or burning my fingers. The Moon was as near as the hand I held it in, and a good deal smaller. Hills and trees and houses were right up to me, and they came in all sizes (some tinier than my thumbnail and others bigger than my whole body) and those sizes kept changing. How big the planes on the ground were, and how tiny the planes in the sky! And how very tiny the people in them had to be! Distant children (wrongly so-called) weren't full-size children way over there: they were pigmy children, pleasingly quiet and well-behaved, right here. Fierce dogs, so long as they stayed no bigger than mice and barked in whispers, weren't a bit frightening. All told, it wasn't so much that I lived in a world of wonderfully elastic things as that they lived in me as my very own. I had nothing to push them out with. To see a flower was to flower. To smell it was to smell like that. The blue of the bright blue sky was the blue of my shining face. Only that wicked sneak-thief called Distance was, as yet, distant from me.

You could say that I was omnipresent. Or, less flatteringly, that my world at that time was shallow, paper-thin, two-dimensional. But you couldn't deny that the thinness was actual-factual, firmly based on the evidence. (After all, what anyone – even a grown-up – sees he sees where he is, not over there where he locates that object.) It was as if I put my stars, like celestial greyhounds, on leads which I pulled so tight that the length of each lead, viewed end-on, shrank to a point.

But I was as deep as my world was shallow. Grounded on and coming from the fathomless Ground of my Being, I drew on immense interior resources. No wonder I made more progress on one of those early days than in months and years later on. And the secret of my success was that I wasn't a bit what I looked like. I was unbounded clear space for my world to happen in. The fact that I had no way of passing on the good news didn't make it less good or less true. Quite the reverse. People called me small and themselves big. Little did they know!

But how brief was my immensity!

The Fall

Suddenly I collapsed, fell away from things, lost touch with them. Distance, coming between me and my treasures, robbed me of them all. Now for the first time I knew about depth. But alas it was no longer mine and within me and supportive, but theirs and outside me and oppressive. I had been so profound and my world so shallow, and now all was reversed. Almost overnight the one who had been omnipresent became omni-absent. The world that had been lost in me had all-at-once become the world I was lost in. And I can't exaggerate the difference this come-down made to my world and myself.

The changes in me and in my world were intertwined. My dear little twinkling stars rushed off to become vast infernos of superheated gasses, light-years away, and certainly they were the last things I owned or wished to own. Now I had no way of shrinking bad-tempered dogs and difficult children and bossy adults to manageable proportions, or of expanding the nice ones. They all stayed the same size, whatever their distance. There is the rose and here am I, and I know of no machinery for bringing us together. And so it goes. I'm lonely and I'm small, a stranger in a strange land. I used to fill to the rafters the biggest church or railway station or airport, comfortably incorporating all those funny people. I was their cheerfully uninspectable inspector. Now I'm everybody's inspectee, floored, shrunken, anxiously traipsing around in their midst. What a come-down!

It's impossible to do justice to the contrast between my original state and my fallen state, between the ease and freedom of the former and the unease (or disease) and constraint of the latter. And perhaps the worst thing about my fallen state is that all-too-soon it masquerades as my natural and normal condition, and a great improvement on what faint recollections I have of my childish inclusiveness and at-largeness, Few of us have any idea how low we have sunk.

To tell the sad story in the old vivid way, Lucifer was the brightest and topmost angel in Heaven, but he fell. He wasn't pushed, he jumped. Distancing himself from heavenly things and clutching us humans in his headlong descent, he landed in Hell. In the deepest Pit where each is his own and on his own and separated from the others by an unbridgeable gap. Up there in Heaven I'm one with you, down here in Hell I'm one without you and we are forever two. Our fall was our mutual distancing and multiplication. Our salvation is our coming together again into oneness with the One.

Salvation

I who had been so kindly deep, and whose world had been so kindly shallow, had become the one who was now so unkindly shallow and whose world had become so unkindly deep. I became desperate. I touched bottom.

And then (and only then) a voice saying to me: "You certainly need saving, and you certainly are saved. The great and uplifting work is accomplished. You have only to come to your senses and look, to see that you are already in Heaven."

So I looked to see, making a point of starting again with the childlike and entertaining and light-hearted things, before moving on to the sublimities of Heaven. Why? Why because Heaven isn't only fun but funny serious, whereas Hell is humourless and heavy and deadly serious.

I don't have to mount to the top of the Empire State Building, or go hang-gliding or helicopting, to get back my toy cars, or my swarms of Lilliputians on the sidewalk. All I have to do, down in the street, is to wake up to the fact that the cars and the people are all the while magically expanding and contracting, the cars swiftly, the people slowly. As for the buildings, how they twist and turn as they swell and shrink! I'm amazed that I should have hallucinated otherwise, and dreamt that I lived in a world that had ground to a halt and stopped dancing for joy, in a rigidly *standardised* world of huge mountains, big hills, fairly large trees and houses, smallish people, and tiny creepy-crawlies. What a hidebound, kill-joy, police-run country Hell is! I'm astounded that I should ever have pictured my before-the-fall condition as silly and handicapping and my after-the-fall condition as sensible and practical. Why didn't I realise much sooner than I did that the reason for my fear and loneliness and lostness and awkwardness was my blindness, my rejection in Hell of what I saw in favour of what Old Nick, who is the Father of Lies, told me to see?

The facts are favourable, lies aren't. The risen or saved life isn't just different from the old fallen life but in all important respects its diametric opposite. At the mouth of the well once more, you are a deep one all right, possessed of infinite interior resources, while up here you are at the marvellous Centre of a marvellous Cosmos, the Centre that has gobbled up all its radii! It's this abolition of radial distance in Heaven`which makes all the difference, and ensures that the barriers are down and you give place to the other, and in truth give your life for the other – because it's your Nature to do so.

In the beginning there was Depth. It wasn't only safely stowed away in you and wonderfully resourceful, but like the deep blue sea it buoyed you up along with your treasure-fleet. Then you fell overboard and sank to the bottom of the sea, so that all its depth was on top of you and your treasure-fleet was pirated. And then, just in time, you were rescued and hauled to the surface, and once more the captain of your fleet.

The good Depth that became the bad Depth has become the good Depth again. You are saved, and saved absolutely.

13

ADVENTURES IN THE REAL WONDERLAND

Do you understand the depth of this mystery?
Man who is so little among the visible creatures,
a shadow and a dustgrain, possesses in the
centre of his being God in His entirety.
St. Symeon the New Theologian (949-1020)

Periodically we take a break from our business or professional anxieties and status, and how necessary this is! Could it be even more necessary to take frequent holidays from our *human* anxieties and status? Are such get-aways conceivable, let alone feasible? Or are we in fact as much prisoners of our humanhood as a snail is of its snailhood, or a dung-beetle is of its dung-beetlehood? And, in spite of all our cleverness, quite incapable of arriving at an objective and impartial view of our condition, much less of taking a break from that condition?

That's the question we are going to address here. As I see it, it's *the* question. To shift one's viewpoint from an all-too-human position to an extra-human (and presumably extraterrestrial) station – a shift guaranteed genuine by the huge *physical* changes it necessitates in the viewer – now that would be something to write home about! Not this time Alice's adventures in an imaginary wonderland but our very own Adventures in the Real Wonderland! In God's Wonderland, you might say.

But I doubt whether we shall get anywhere near this far-flung goal, or much further at all, until we are clear about where we now stand. To break out of jail, first know your jail. We begin, accordingly, by examining, with what honesty and detachment we can muster at this early stage, our human condition. Only then is there the remotest chance (let's rank it no higher than that) of taking a holiday from that condition.

I pick on the following five characteristics. If they seem to you unacceptably disagreeable, why that's exactly what they are. And the sooner we admit it the brighter are our chances of breaking through to a saner and happier land or wonderland.

Loneliness

You and I are shut up in little boxes with the lids shut tight and padlocked. Or let's say: here we are, I in my small prison and you in yours, peering cautiously at each other through two tiny and frequently bunged-up peep-holes in the wall of our prison cell. Each is sentenced to solitary life-imprisonment under conditions that couldn't be more stringent and lonesome. For instance, I have no way of knowing whether you or any other prisoner (and there are countless billions of us) experience anything like the sensations of touch, taste, smell, and vision that I experience. And, of course, there's the still more disturbing realisation that these prison walls are as thought-proof and feeling-proof as they are sensation-proof. We are all strangers by nature. And what is Hell but all-round estrangement and alienation?

Confrontation

We humans are pitted against each other. Our prison cells are set up that way, each opposite to and opposed to its neighbour. And inseparable from the physical fact is the feeling, and inseparable from the feeling is the behaviour. Confrontation is the rule in all departments: not only you or me versus him or her, but parents versus children and vice versa, male versus female and vice versa, the old versus the young and vice versa, religion v. religion, ideology v. ideology, nation v. nation, and so on and on. What option do we have? This is our life.

Death

It's a life that passes in a flash. Not only am I a grounded and wingless mayfly that's well aware of how ephemeral it is and how far advanced in the process of dying, but a mayfly that's scared out of its wits. And, stemming from my fear of death and eternal oblivion, are the countless fears that proliferate from that dark root.

Restlessness

To say that we humans are fidgety and ill-at-ease and restless is a grotesque understatement. Suffering the punishment of the guilty lovers Paolo and Francesca in Dante's Inferno, we are blown hither and thither by relentless and cruel winds. Longing for peace and stillness, we are forever on the go, driven.

Lostness

My fantasy is that the fellow I am is of some consequence in the Universe, that he amounts to something in the Scheme of Things. My fate is that he is of no consequence and amounts to nothing. I'm utterly lost in the unimaginably vast expanses of cosmic time and space. What could be more insignificant, its life and struggles and agony and death more meaningless, more futile, than yours and mine, cast against our wishes into this howling wilderness?

In sum, then, to be a human being is to be lonely, pitted against the other humans, dying, driven, and lost.

This inescapable truth is so painful that we suppress it by all available means. And, on those occasions when we can no longer sweep it under the carpet of consciousness, we apply it to others and not ourselves. Most of us succeed in drugging ourselves into an uninterrupted stupor. Our well-stocked pharmacy of anaesthetics and opiates includes some forms of religion, a 300-page novel a week (which is a fictional life for escaping from real life), beer, hyperactivity, telly soap every night, compulsive shopping every day, the travel that narrows the mind, the lifelong enjoyment of ill health, and so on and on. Anything myopic will do. But of course, to suppress is to empower. The sure way to suffer the full brunt of our human handicaps – all five of the primary ones I've listed, plus countless secondary ones – is so to structure our every waking moment that awareness of those handicaps is crowded out. Dumped into the shadowy underworld where they constitute the stuff our nightmares are made of.

In fact, of course, there's no escape. We are human, and our humanness isn't just like that. It is that. Which does not mean that there's nothing we can do about it.

What we can do, and what we are about to do here, is this. Having at last directed the searchlight of consciousness onto our human condition, we turn up the candlepower. In other words we look more attentively and honestly into the one who's looking, and for a change we see what we see, instead of what wishful and fearful thinking and language and Big Brother tells us to see. The result is that we make some surprising discoveries.

For some of us this most challenging and crucial of enterprises has a communal and public side as well as a personal and private side. My friends and I meet in get-togethers (I hate the term workshops) where we try out and practise the new way of life and the new sort of personal relationships that follow from our discoveries. But here on paper, of course, you and I have to find another way of doing exactly the same thing together.

It turns out to be (I'm as surprised as you are) the comic-strip method. With this difference: in the following 11-frame strip-cartoon I'm not, like Asterix or Tintin, seeking to amuse or instruct you, but to get you to devote at least half-an-hour of your valuable time to research, to the most fundamental and do-or-die research of all. To be precise, half the pictures require your careful attention, the other half your careful attention and action. Thirty minutes, please!

A word of warning here. If you think you know what it would be like if you did the things I ask you to do, and therefore can't be bothered to comply, I promise you no adventures and no wonder-land, but only puzzlement and annoyance and boredom.

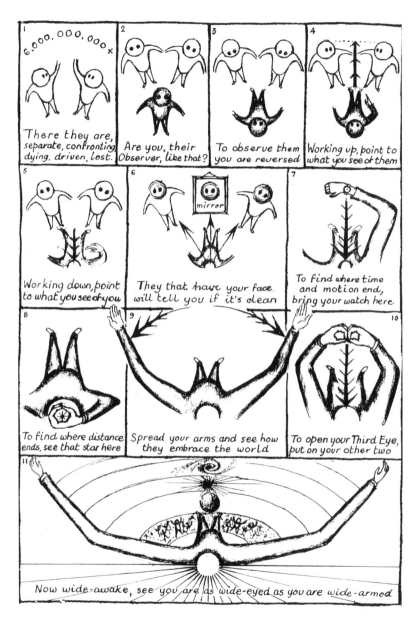

Well, what happened? Did you find yourself undergoing transformation, stage by clear-cut stage, from that tiny human perisher in frame 2 into the unbounded Immortal in frame 11? In other words, did you switch from what you look like to others over there to what you are for yourself at Centre? And were you duly impressed by the difference between these two versions of yourself? If so, my heartfelt congratulations! Please read on, skipping the next paragraph.

If parts or the whole of our 11-stage investigation made no sense to you, please give it another try, this time more slowly. And if this doesn't work, please now go through the Notes at the end of this chapter. I think they will help.

The time has come for you who have successfully carried out our research project, along with myself who set it up, to take stock.

You will remember how we began by wondering whether it's possible to take a holiday from our human condition. And how we went on to admit just how desperate that condition is, and how much-needed that holiday. And we had a very serious go at shifting our Centre and Viewpoint to an extra-human and indeed extra-terrestrial location – a shift so huge that we could be sure was real only if it necessitated and brought about drastic *physical* changes (along with every other sort of change) in the viewer. Universally verifiable changes, let's add.

Well, those physical changes have certainly happened, and they are certainly drastic, and any open-minded inquirer can check them anywhere and anytime. Just compare the little one we started with in frame 2 with the immense One we arrived at in frame 11! The contrast is total. And it's the latter and not the former that you and I see that we are looking out of now and always, whose Centre coincides with yours and mine. We *have* that little human, but we *are* this immense Supra-human. That little one's not for putting down or denying, but for placing and treasuring – out there in the realm of things that are born and change and die. This we do by virtue of our union with the No-thing they are born out of, and die back into, right Here.

We have arrived at these revolutionary conclusions, please note, by wholly secular means, by looking to see what's actually on show instead of what society tells us is on show, by kowtowing to the Data rather than Authority. No holy book and no holy guru or cleric crept into our comic strip. Nevertheless I think you'll agree that our strictly lay and contemporary comedy merges nicely with the Divine Comedy of the world's great spiritual traditions. For instance, I can hear you saying, if you happen to be an Advaitist, "Yes, my Third Eye is wide open, and it's the Eye of the One without a second, the One I Am." Or, if you happen to be a Buddhist, "Like the Buddha I take myself to no outside refuge. I cannot by *going* reach the Place where there's no birth, no ageing, no death, no rebirth." Or, if you are a Muslim, "As the Prophet says, Allah is nearer to me than my own neck-vein." Or, if you are a Christian, "Like Paul, it's not I who live but Christ Who lives in me. These arms that embrace the world – whose are they but His? This Light and Love at my very Core – are they not mine solely by virtue of my union with the One Who is Light and Love?"

And when our own most private and recent and secular discoveries dovetail with the most universal and ancient and sacred discoveries of our race, we are surely onto a Good Thing. If their combined message isn't for writing on our hearts and living by, tell me what is.

Well, however heavy your religious payload may be (or however much of it you may have jettisoned) you have, fuelled by the grace of the One (as some of us would put it), rocketed from a mundane and commonplace launch-pad to what is surely the most wonderful of Wonderlands.

How can you be quite sure of and enjoy your arrival here?

I know of only one way. It is by finding out how, day by day and minute by minute, this rocket that loses part of itself in flight and re-models the rest – this leap that transforms the leaper – deals with the five basic troubles he suffers from on the ground, Let's take those endemic human sicknesses one by one, and see how they yield to this most dynamic of treatments.

Loneliness

Inso*far* as I am that coloured, textured, opaque something, that small closed-up fellow of frame 2 who visibly has no room for anyone or anything else, why of course I'm just that something, and as all-exclusive very much alone. But inso*near* and inas*much* as I really am this colourless, untextured, transparent Nothing, this opened-up fellow of frame 11, who visibly has unlimited room for everyone and everything else, why of course I am them, and as all-inclusive very much alone once again. Either way – whether as that little one in frames 2 and 3 and 4, or as this big one in frame 11 – I'm on my own. But there's a difference. In my human (lack of) capacity I'm alone by exclusion, while in my supra-human capacity I'm alone by inclusion. In fact, none other than the Alone. And the perfect antidote for my human loneliness is my divine Aloneness.

The way this works out for me in practice is this. I used to locate what I called *my consciousness* in Douglas Harding, to claim it as the private property of that fellow in frame 2. In other words, his frightful loneliness was of his own making. But now, coming to my senses, I shift Centre to the fellow in frame 11, to the Consciousness of the One Who is the One Consciousness. And I find that, to the extent that I stay centred here, all that fuss about the loneliness of the long-term prisoner melts away, and I have all the "telepathic and clairvoyant" access to the experience of others that I need. All I can do with from moment to moment, no more and no less. And to you I say: go on making that one-metre (but astronomical) leap from the lonely to the Alone and see for yourself how it lands you in the heart of all creatures, via the Heart of their Creator.

Confrontation

There's no way we humans – we wee humans – can avoid confrontation. You see we are set up face-to-face, you hear us saying so (whoever heard talk of face-to-space?), you observe and endure its manifold consequences. There's evidence for you, in triplicate! But in the wings there waits another witness, eager to testify. As this witness you swear that you personally, in sharp contrast to those innumerable human witnesses, belong to another species, another genus, another order of being altogether. Looking right now at What you are Where you are, you see that never, not for a split second, have you confronted or could confront anyone or anything, not your worst enemy or best friend, not the dog or the cat or any other creature. No matter how loving or courteous, humans as such cannot vanish in favour of anybody, whereas the One they really are can't do otherwise. In Christian language, the awesome truth is that at your heart is the self-giving Love that dies for the world and for you.

Death

Sooner or later every thing is unthinged. In all the regions where you amount to something or other, you are a perishing something or other. But at Centre, where What sees consciously vanishes in favour of what's seen, you are No-thing whatever. And where there's No-thing there's nothing to change, and where there's nothing to change there's no change and no way of registering time, and no time to register (frame 7). Only stay alive to your timeless and imperishable Core, and along with your fear of Death will die all its frightful progeny. Or let me put it like this: if you would rather not die, remember that you are offered union with the only One that won't die.

Restlessness

Every thing is unquiet, unstable, on the move, shackled to the spokes of the wheel of birth and maturing and ageing and death. Forever pinpointed at the Axis of that wheel, you are the No-thing that never budged a nanometer. Thus you have seen (frame 7) how the motion of the hands of your watch, as well as the time they indicate, and indeed the watch itself, vanishes on really close inspection. And from now on, at the wheel of your car, in the train or the plane, you have only to look to see that here you really are the Unmoved Mover of the world that's the other side of the glass. Everything there, from the stars downwards, is visibly on the move in your Stillness, and the nearer it is the faster it goes. Can you think of a more adventurous adventure than this?

Lostness

We have seen how, as a human being, you amount to less than a dustgrain in the Cosmos, how hopelessly you are lost in its vastness. Yes, but we have also seen how, as the One you really are, the Cosmos is lost – and found – in you. Those Wide-opened Arms of yours enfold all creatures great and small. And your Single Eye takes in a hundred constellations as comfortably as a candle-flame. No doubt living the wide-open, wide-armed, wide-eyed way is going to need much practice. But it helps to remember that it's the natural way of life for relaxing into now, not an ideal way of life for achieving in some distant future.

Well, I hope we have come up with enough, in words and pictures and things to do – enough to show how thoroughly your supra-humanness can cope with and take care of your human-ness, if you will allow it to do so. How What you are centrally is the much-needed medicine for and completion of what you are peripherally, how you are rescued from your manifold miseries and delinquencies by the infinite Power of the Goodness that in its entirety lives in your very heart, and how this ever-renewed discovery of yours is no solemn and Sunday observance smothered in pious dust and anaesthetic blah-blah-blah, but your thrilling and never-ending Adventure in the Real Wonderland.

I'm not saying, mind you, that a life consciously lived from its true Centre will be safe or painless, easy or consistently joyful. Real adventure is made of sterner stuff. Those great arms embrace the suffering of the world no less than its splendour and its thrill. Those hands know the torment of crucifixion. Only so can the terrible pain of the world be overcome. The real joy, the joy that casts no shadow and knows no variation, has come through the fire. In our depths dwells the great Risk-taker, the bravest, the most daring, the toughest, the wildest and the most shocking as well as the most triumphant of adventurers. What is our comic strip, what is the Divine Comedy itself, without the Divine Comedian, without its astounding Star and Impresario? I see this chapter as one of His countless love-letters to you and to me, inviting us to let go and have a go with Him. Or rather – marvel of marvels and mercy of mercies – *as* Him!

Notes

If the message of our strip-cartoon is so unfamiliar to you that in places it's nonsensical, or if its message is so familiar to me that I have so far failed to make it clear, then I believe these notes will help.

Let's work through the cartoon's 11 frames one by one.

1. I don't pick on these five unhappy aspects of our human condition only because they are so miserable. I have another reason. They are also those we turn a blind eye to, in spite of the fact that, when at long last we dare to look into them, we find they don't really apply to us at all!

2. The basic human delusion is that one is much the same, whether viewed from over there by others (and by oneself "through their eyes") or from here by oneself.

3. If you find it difficult to see that you are the other way up than the person you are facing, try this. Hold up a level forearm and, slowly bringing it down, observe above it ('resting' on it) his or her head, neck, trunk, legs, feet, in that order. Then your feet, legs, trunk, in that reverse order.

4. Now I'm asking you to point to what you see of him or her, to what's coloured and textured and opaque, slowly working *up* this time, from footwear to hair-do.

5. Now repeat the operation on yourself, again starting with your feet. When you come to the place where your shirt/blouse/pullover fades from sight, *outline with your touching forefinger the semicircular left-shoulder-to-right-shoulder Frontier where the colour and texture and opacity of that garment (along with your fingernail) fade away.* And, warned by Zen Master Huang-Po that the wise go by what they see and the foolish by what they think they see, respect that Frontier from now on.

In the following frames we examine the extraordinary functions of the colourless, textureless, transparent Space beyond the Frontier, the Space you are looking out of.

6.   What has happened to its 'occupier', to that most cared-for and cared-about of your possessions – to that coloured and textured and opaque object you call your face? It has broken loose and set up on its own over there, about one metre from the Frontier. But it's no mere apparition haunting the air around you. It has found a home, many homes from home. Your mirror is one of them, but those two fellows are equally hospitable. Unlike you, they are in a position to say whether you have a smut on your cheek, or egg on your beard.

7.   Different places have different times, and when you go there you check what *the time is* by consulting clocks and watches. To find out what the time is at Home when you visit you, you bring your watch right up to your Eye – only to discover that here *the time isn't* ! Intrinsically you are timeless.

8.   What you see you see Where and When you are. It's only when its light gets all the way to you that you register that object. Each star is visibly distant from other stars, but none of them is distant from you! In fact, you are omnipresent!

9.   Try embracing the scene, no matter how wide it is, with these arms of yours. You will find they leave nothing out. Now try to find anyone who's anything like as wide-armed as you.

10. Are you wearing glasses? I bet you the price of this book that, on the contrary, you are wearing a monocle! To fit your Single Eye.

11. Finally, take off your monocle, thus turning it into glasses again. But make sure you remain a Cyclops. With your hands try to find the limits of the Single Eye you are looking out of. If you can't, it's because its Owner is limitless.

14

BELIEF IN GOD

I find it difficult to believe in God. And certainly in the orthodox God, in God as advertised, in the official God, or let's say in God as He's taken to be by most sensible people.

Here are my reasons.

1. It seems that, rather like Gravity or a sort of Holy Gas, He's all over the place, everywhere in general and nowhere in particular. Which makes Him hard to find, to pin down.

2. Equally, it seems, He's timeless, spread all over history and nowhen in particular. Which makes Him hard to date, to fix an appointment with.

3. And, of course, He's perfectly invisible. Which makes Him much harder to take seriously than the people and things around me, to take seriously at all.

4. All of which underscores the belief – so built-in it goes without saying – that He's pure Spirit and therefore bodiless. And how smoothly "He's no body" slithers over into "He's nobody"!

5. "Bodiless" certainly means "brainless" and "brainless" is usually taken to mean "mindless". A conclusion that recent sages such as Ramana and Nisargadatta and D.T. Suzuki (to say nothing of the behaviourist psychologists J.B. Watson and B.F. Skinner) confirm when they tell me that the trouble with my mind is

that I think I have one, or am one. To which I would add that God isn't likely to be burdened with a load that I may free myself of. How then can I avoid the conclusion that He's as mindless as He's bodiless? Or perhaps it would be safer to say that His mind – if any – must be so different from mine that it should be called something else. Which in practice – in my practice at least – is surely enough to put the lid on His unreality.

6. I find it as difficult to believe in an impersonal God who's so unlike me that He's unimaginable as to believe in a personal God who's so like me that He's all-too-imaginable and so obviously a projection of mine, an anthropomorph. Either way I'm agnostic.

7. And I find it as difficult to believe in an unloving and callous God, who in this respect at least is my inferior, as to believe in a loving God who seemingly does so little to relieve undeserved suffering. Either way, again, I'm agnostic.

Well, I don't know about you, but such are my reasons for doubting God's existence. They add up to quite a case. Is it any wonder that the modern world has no time for Him?

Am I then a Godforsaking and Godforsaken unbeliever, an atheist, albeit a reluctant atheist? Have I really got rid of Him? Will He forever head my list of Missing Persons?

The doubt won't go away: maybe He's not a bit like that, and my provisional Identikit is wrong on all seven counts, even a sure guide to what He's not like!

Let's see. Let's take those seven reasons for agnosticism and see how they stand up to inspection.

(1) Where is He?

I start with the challenging fact that, sparsely scattered through-out the history of the great religions, there have been men and women (and they include an exceptionally gifted bunch of poets as well as saints and sages) who claim to locate God exactly. To pinpoint Him as precisely as if He were the hardest-to-catch and most gorgeous of butterflies. In all this immense Universe, they say, there's just one Spot, one Point, one infinitesimal Door that opens on that vastest of palaces where He awaits you and me.

So they say. Let's give precision and punch to their message by applying it to our present situation. The spot they speak so highly of is none other than the place where you can no longer see your shirt-front – blouse, pullover, whatever – where it fades from view, the Spot marked Y (Y for you, my Reader) in our picture. Here and here alone, they assure us, He's to be found.

According to these authorities, then, this favourite Place of His, so far from being the hardest place to locate and get to, is the easiest place to locate and get to. But to make sure that this is indeed the Place, we need to know what is the Time, the right moment to call on Him and discover whether those authorities know what they are talking about.

(2) When is He at Home?

The same folk who tell us precisely where to find Him tell us precisely when to find Him. In effect they say: throughout all the vast time-span of the Universe there's just one moment when you'll catch Him in and waiting to greet you.

And when is that?

Just glance at your wristwatch. It tells you the exact time of your appointment with Him. At all other times He's out on business. And, what's still more remarkable, only He is right here and now at Y, only He is with you and present in both senses of the word. All others and all else, including the scene indicated in our picture, are absentees, are so many Xs hanging out over there. And what's there is then, if only because the light you see it by takes time to get to you at Y.

Here, again, notice how drastically our initial Identikit is

117

reversed. The One that was taken to be the great Absconder, impossible to catch up with, turns out to be the closest, the only One that won't go away!

Or so they tell us. We must now check for ourselves whether they tell the truth, by actually looking to see what's on show at Point Y.

(3) Is He Visable?

Here again is the picture, with additions.

You could call it your map, the map of your 30cm journey from X to Y, a trip that's not so much an excursion as an incursion. You make that journey for dear life (it's the most real and decisive journey you

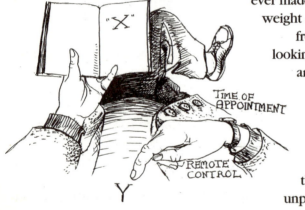

ever made) by shifting the weight of your attention from what you are looking at to what you are looking out of, from these printed words and this letter X to what's taking them in at Y – the unprintable Y on the transparency that you see you are, of course, not the printed Y on my opaque attempt to draw what you see.

Please point to the former, and go on doing so.

You are pointing at the Door that (like your garage door at home?) is conveniently opened by Remote Control, namely your in-pointing forefinger, as indicated in the illustration.

Observe what, on present evidence, is being pointed at, what is most central to you, your home-ground, the place you are coming from. Not at what you think or believe or are told or feel you are looking out of, but at what you actually see. Take your time, and slowly, slowly, slowly, with total attention, check whether Door Y automatically opens to reveal what is:

- Boundless, extending in all directions to Infinity,
- Transparent, spotless, empty,
- Not empty for empty but empty for filling with whatever's currently on offer, as roughly indicated on my drawing,
- The changeless and therefore timeless and imperishable Receptacle of all perishing things, the eternal Playground of all Time's children.
- Later on, at the wheel of your car, the Unmoved Mover of the landscape and skyscape.

Please continue in-pointing.

Now if, entering by this nearest and smallest but best of doors, you clearly see the One who (to sum up) is Boundless, Empty, Full, and Deathless, and Who in you is wide-wide-wide awake to Himself as all this, why then you know you have found Him, the One and only One, at your very heart.

"You have the right to speak of God," says Ramakrishna, "only after you have seen Him." Provided you have carried out the foregoing investigation with sufficient inquisitiveness and care, and found for sure the characteristics I asked you to look for, you have earned that right. What's more, knowing exactly where to look for Him, and exactly when, and exactly how, and exactly what to look for, you can now *at will* see Him at your very Centre and Source. And, what's still more, you can at will see that *only* He is always to hand, *only* He is present when you need Him most and others least. Only He!

Now I put it to you that this seeing of the Perfect One at your core is instantaneous and perfect seeing. That to see Him at all is to see Him all at once and as He is, and that there are no blurred or partial sightings of your Origin. How different it is when you view Its products! Take for instance those hands of yours, one holding this book and the other pointing at its Reader. However long and carefully you study this scene – the hugely complex texture-range and colour-range and patterning of these familiar objects – you miss most of it and quickly forget what you did get. Moreover you left out the other side and the inside of those things, the hierarchy of little things they consist of and the big things they depend on, and without which they aren't even surfaces, aren't anything at all. So I say: things are too complex and too missing, too scattered in time and place, to be seen. At best, they are glimpsed. Only the Awake No-thing which is the God who is perfectly simple and altogether present (present in two – no, three! – senses of that portmanteau word) can be perfectly seen, can be seen at all, strictly speaking. And who but Himself can see Himself?

Yes, to see Him is to be Him. Such is the generosity, the gracious hospitality of the King of Kings that all His guests are presented with and lit up with His very own Eye, the Eye that sees Him and all things in Him. Look now, you that have made that more-than-Olympic leap from X to Y, look again at what you are looking out of, at what's taking in these printed words. At Y you have opened the Eye that sees itself as unique and single, as wider than the wide world, and gifted with the divine power of destroying and re-creating the world. (People will tell you that all you are doing is closing and opening a pair of tiny peep-holes in a very human topknot. But you know better. People are much too far off to see what's going on here.)

In brief, then, so far from being invisible, He alone is altogether visible, thanks to the superb gift and birthday present of His very own Eye. What price our precious Identikit now?

However the question crops up: does this clear vision of Him as No-thing whatever mean that He's altogether discarnate, airy-fairy, gone-with-the-wind? I confess I'm in no hurry to take on board, let alone take on board as my Pilot, a Breeze, no matter how refreshing and sail-filling it may be.

(4) Has He a Body?

Is it possible that here at last our Identikit has got it right? Who but a savage (I ask myself), or a psychotic, or a deplorably super-stitious devotee could presume to decant Him who is 100% pure Spirit into any sort of vessel or container or mould?

Again, let's see.

It might be a good idea to start with you, my Reader, who I have every reason to suppose are built in God's image, and therefore could furnish clues to His embodiment or lack of it. To start with, let's face the fact that without other humans your body isn't a human body: feral children, brought up by animals, aren't human. That without the living bodies it lives on your body isn't alive. That without the astronomical bodies it lives in it's a total write-off: you could survive for decades the amputation of all four limbs and much else, but how long could you survive the amputation of your Sun? Ask yourself what it takes to be what you are, then tell me what astronomical and terrestrial and human and infrahuman level, along with its inhabitants, you can leave out of your reckoning. What is the True Body of all these bodies that comprise this exquisitely close-knit Universe in which we all make a living by taking in one another's washing, in which (to speak plainly) everything depends on and conditions everything else? What is it but – the Universe? Nothing less will do. You aren't all there (as we say) till you are All Here, the Whole of things, the one strictly Indivisible Body which is your very own Physique. By no means yours in your human capacity, of course, but in union with the One you really are at Centre and Circumference. To put it another way, there's only One Body, of which all bodies are *disjecta membra*, or rather organs and organelles. And in (rightly and explicitly) claiming to be embodied you are (rightly and implicitly) claiming to be Him. Just think of how the sustained enjoyment of this fact (which lies hidden in the very foundation of science) could change your life in the world! Into your life as the world!

Yes, for the fourth time our Identikit has been up-ended. We were asking if He had or was a body. The answer is No! Not on your life. He is THE Body. The No-thing is Every-thing. And if you tell me this Body is too moribund and too messy to be His, I'll refer you to the fabled fly that, crawling over a Rembrandt, was appalled at those huge dirt-coloured patches; until, taking off, he took in the whole picture.

But the question remains: what's the good, what's the point of this colossal masterpiece of a Body if it has no mind to match, no Mind of Its Own?

(5) Has He a Mind?

Let's begin by taking a quick look at what we call your mind. Again, you shall be the clue to You.

You and I know how "narrow-minded" we inevitably are. How what we experience is the tiniest fragment of all that's there for the experiencing. Now instead of reading this "narrowness" as a liability for deploring, let's try reading it as an asset for welcoming, a necessity. How, I ask you, could you live your life and have a mind of your own if you were always being swamped by what's going on in my mind, in all those other minds? Isn't there an immense amount of mindstuff that you don't wish to know, wish not to know, can't afford to know?

Yes of course, I think you'll agree. But this does not mean that the great world of mental goings-on is closed to you, isn't for drawing on as and when required.

Consider the well-documented and partially verified facts of ESP – including telepathy, clairvoyance, precognition, recollection of past lives, etc. – to say nothing of our ordinary sensitivity to the moods of people and the feel of places. Consider also what saints get up to. The penitents of the Curé d'Ars (that God-centred priest) didn't need to tell him all that was happening in their minds and lives: he knew enough of it anyway to do his job wonderfully well. Now I ask you: what do all such paranormal phenomena point steadily to? What but One Mind to go with that One Body? What but a bottomless Reservoir of know-what and know-how for us all to tap as and when needed? And (what's equally important) to turn off as and when not needed?

The truth is that we are all connected to the Main. Each of us, more or less well-plumbed, is fitted with a valve that lets in as much of the General Pool of Mindstuff as we can do with moment by moment. In fact, just as we found that in the last resort there's only one Body, so we are finding that there's only One Mind to go with it; and that together (perfectly distinct yet perfectly united) they comprise the Body-Mind of the One that you and I really, really are. To clinch this vital conclusion, I suggest you try it out. That you observe how your vision of the One opens you more and more to the Many, to all you need to know about them. How it automatically adjusts your valve as required.

Meanwhile it certainly looks as if, so far from being mindless (as our Identikit proposed) the One is marvellously mindful: is, in fact, the strictly indivisible One and Only Mind that ever was or will be. But when we go on to say that – since the whole of your mind is the Mind of the Whole – you may enjoy access to the very thoughts of God, you may well be dubious and somewhat shocked. "My IQ may be high," you protest, "but surely not that high!"

Well, let's see if you pass the following GQ Test.

Of all the piled-up proof that you have indeed put on your jumping shoes and jumped into God (as Eckhart put it) one is paramount. It starts by asking: why is there anything at all? Why is there so much as a twinge or tingle of consciousness, or a speck of a speck of matter? Why isn't there just nothing whatever? Does the miraculous – no, impossible! – uprush of the Self-originating One from primordial chaos and darkest night, without help or reason, hoisting Himself into existence by His own non-existent bootstraps, astound and delight you? If so, I can assure you that it is you as Him, and certainly not you as Jane or Henry or whoever, who are amazed, who are filled with admiration, who jump for joy into that very special joy that's born from that very special and never-ceasing Miracle. The "impossible" Miracle of His Self-creation, after which the creation of billions of universes, all going strong, is nothing special, a matter of routine.

But the ineffable brilliance and mystery of the Self-Originating One could leave us with the feeling that here's a fearsome It rather than a homely He-She, an alien What rather than an approachable Who. Which brings us to the question –

(6) Is God a Person?

Surely His immensity, His purity, His all-inclusiveness, His timelessness and timefullness, His all-moving stillness, His creative and destructive prowess, and above all His useful knack of Self-origination – surely this divine laundry list adds up to such a basketful that we must think of Him as superpersonal or impersonal rather than a person in the sense that Mrs Jones is a person. Or do these characteristics belong to a Being who, notwithstanding all that splendour, you can call your Friend, and confide in, and ask forgiveness of, and crack jokes with, and get help from, and lean back on, and love so much that your dearest wish is to lose yourself in Him?

Let's spare a moment to look at what we mean by personhood. In daily life, as in grammar, we distinguish three sorts of persons. That fellow over there, as such, is a third person. You who face me, as such, are a second person. I, the one right here that's taking him and you in, am a first person. As such, I'm centered upon and operating from Point Y of our picture. Accordingly I say: over there he IS, facing me you ARE, right here I AM.

This I AM, this First Person, is always and only Singular, and in truth there's no First Person plural. Strictly speaking, the word WE, though socially indispensable, is a trap and a blindfold, the most potent and addictive of halucinogens. Take, for example, the statement: *we are tasting wine*. The implication that you and I are doing the same thing is false. What's happening on present evidence is that *that* glass of wine is disappearing into a lip-and-tooth-lined hole in the vicinity of X where it remains tasteless, whereas *this* glass of wine is disappearing into a lipless and toothless Abyss at Point Y where it's for tasting. And if you happened to be hosting all the wet-lipped wine drinkers of the world you would still be the only Lipless Taster, the solitary Y among all those Xs. As First Person Singular you are singular-peculiar as well as singular-unitary. And your wine is doubly sacramental since it not only celebrates but seals your union with the One, the Alone.

In reality, as Meister Eckhart pointed out, only God has the right to say I. And when I do so it is by grace and courtesy of my oneness with the One who is the Unique First Person Singular, Present Tense. And when I take you and others to be persons also, I recognise implicitly that your personhood is His, on loan or franchise, so to say, from Him to you. Apart from Him we are all unpersons, out of touch with one another, strangers and afraid. George MacDonald was so right when he said that "only in God can man meet man".

We were asking whether God is a person. The answer is No! He is THE Person. He is the First and the Last and the Only Person that is or was or shall be. It follows that the only way to be a person is to be Him. Once again our Identikit, so sure that you and I are persons and so unsure whether God is a person, couldn't have got it more wrong!

A further question. Granted that He is The Person, is He the sort of person that you can experience companionship as well as union with? Can you enjoy Him as more You than you, yet essentially other than you?

Continue putting on your jumping shoes and jumping that 30cm jump from X to Y into His Joy, and see how your relationship with Him develops. You may get some hint of what it will be when you read the lives of the saints. You'll find men and women chatting to God more freely and more frequently than to the folk around them. Paradoxically (and everything at this level is paradoxical) the more sustained their union with Him the more relaxed and lightsome their intimacy with Him as the Adorable Confidant, the truly Bosom Friend. But don't believe them or me. Find out for yourself. Practise, practise, practise jumping for joy – for present joy, not for future joys – into His Joy, and see for yourself.

But that joy would only be complete if it were also love, love jumping for love into His Love. So let's ask –

(7) Is He Loving?

Is He cold or is He caring? Or (wonder of wonders!) is He the Power and the Glory back of the world Who's also the Saviour of the world, the Love that dies so that you and I may live? Were our evangelising forefathers right, after all?

To settle this, my last and burning question, let's take a good look at what's going on over there, in that human region of many Xs, and then compare it with what's going on right here at Y, in this Centre which is God's dwelling place.

We have only to look to see that CONFRONTATION is the most basic and the most obligatory of the games we people play. And we have only to listen to hear ourselves saying that we do indeed stand FACE-TO-FACE, symmetrically, each on a head-on collision course with his or her opposite number. And for sure we feel and behave accordingly. Naturally opposed, we're stuck like that. There's a saying: if it looks like a duck and quacks like a duck and swims like a duck, it is a duck. By the same token, what we look like and talk like and act like, we are.

We are that. We first persons plural (wrongly so-called) are inescapably and obviously built for confrontation. Not so the First Person Singular. I have only to look to see that here I'm built to another plan and for a different purpose. And that never, not for a split second, have I confronted any creature in my life.

My wife Catherine has just walked into the room where I'm writing this. Yonder, in all its as-it-isness and complexity, is that dear and familiar face, on show in this No-face of mine, in the Simplicity and wide-awake Openness of the One that's right here welcoming her.

This One is doing something that Catherine's husband as such could never do, which is to disappear without trace in her or anyone's favour. Actually to die for her, to die that she may live. I say *die*, but in fact this divine and present death is infinitely deeper and deadlier than any feat of disappearance this fellow as such is capable of. And infinitely deeper and deadlier than the human death that awaits this fellow, who will soon be reduced to 200lbs of highly complex goo for the undertaker to dispose of somehow. Whereas God, being simple and goo-free and irreducible, is already disposed of. Not so much as a stray quark of His remains here to get in Catherine's way. Whether as the Nothing that excludes all or as the All that excludes nothing, the true First Person Singular puts paid to confrontation.

In other words, God alone is built for loving. Self-giving love is His speciality. He's the One and only One that's up to (and down to) the job of deliberately giving His life – His very existence – for you and for me. And now that I find myself following suit and vanishing in Catherine's favour, I do so as united by grace to the Only One Who's great enough and humble enough to be capable of such a perfect act of love.

And the joke – the joke's on me – is that, in my preliminary Identikit, I pictured Him as couldn't-care-less or at least bone-idle on our behalf!

So much, then, for our re-appraisal of what GOD – that much

overloaded and little-understood word – stands for. Of what He's really like, once we accept his pressing invitation to visit Him and see Him for ourselves.

So far from being all over the place and hard to pin-point, He turns out to be the nearest and the dearest, right here and right now, Intimacy itself. So far from being invisible, He turns out to be always brilliantly on display, and there are no partial or obscure or distorted sightings of His Perfect Simplicity. So far from being remote and other-worldly and discarnate, He alone is altogether Incarnate, the Completion and the Whole and the Healing of every-body. So far from being mindless His is the One Mind, the Main we are all on, and back of His incredible know-how-to-do is his impossible know-how-to-Be. So far from being a non-person like Father Christmas, or a person of sorts like Mrs Jones, He turns out to be the true First Person O-so-singular, and to be a person is

to be Him. And finally, so far from being indifferent to our distress, He turns out to be the One Who descends from highest heaven to the very sink and cellar of His world, coming to Nought and dying there the deepest of deaths for you and me, for us all. His para-doxical but perfect answer to the question that racks our lives – to be or not to be – is in Him and as Him to be *and* not to be. He that loses his life shall save it.

In short, the One I couldn't believe in has become the only one I can believe in for sure. It's the fellow I thought I was that has become incredible aside from Him. And it's not only the findings of this inquiry but its authorship that has gone into reverse gear, so that the tale told by the indubitable man about the dubitable God has become the tale told by the Indubitable God about the dubitable man!

Nevertheless the hands and arms of that marginal and dubious human are indispensable for carrying out His work in the world. In the tremendous world that these outstretched arms embrace in its entirety.

15

HAPPY
RE-BIRTHDAY

Jesus said:
Truly, truly I say to you, unless a man is born again he
cannot see the Kingdom of God.

Provided you go all the way, and your full development isn't at some stage arrested, you are born again, and again. The grown-up are thrice-born.

The first stage of this progression is, of course, spent in your mother's womb, where in a mere nine months you develop physically from a speck, from a single microscopic cell into a hugely complex multi-cellular animal. Which is then born into the second or social womb, where in a couple of decades you develop psycho-physically from the most incompetent of animals into a multi-competent human being. If all goes well this is followed by your re-birth into the third womb which is the spiritual community, where you develop psycho-spiritually from a merely human being into an awakened being, a being that's alive to Being and Not-Being, a Seer. And finally, at so-called death, you are born into God, into the Cosmic Womb that in truth you never left.

The following illustration will help to pull together the story of our life as a whole, alerting us to our programme, to what's on our

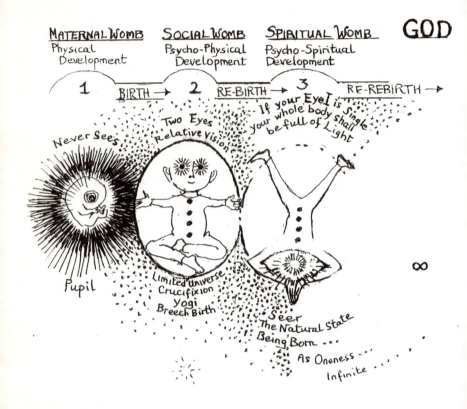

agenda if we are not held up at some stage, if we are not degenerating into cases of arrested development.

I hope that it will also prove useful in the detailed discussion, under the four following heads, which makes up the body of this chapter.

1. Your individual womb-story is the speeded-up version of your ancestral story, its recapitulation.
2. The meaning of each stage is not revealed till the next stage. It's always one jump ahead of itself.
3. At each stage your birth may be by "normal birth-tunnel" means, or else by "caesarean section".
4. Your death is your birth into the Timeless.

(1) Recapitulation

I start with embryology. Of course everyone knows that in one's maternal womb one runs at lightning speed through (say) a billion years of Life's evolution.

Why then (you ask) make a song and dance about it? Because (I reply) *it is, when applied to oneself, the most resisted and hushed up of facts.* I ask you what would happen if, chancing to meet a cheese-mite, or a mosquito, or a spider, you politely took off your hat to a relative whose biological status is way above what yours was not so very long ago? Or saluted a fly as a god or archangel compared with yourself when young? You would be in danger of certification as insane. Or be taken into psychiatric care by so-called sane people who pretend with all their might that they started life in the maternity ward, and will end it in the hospice. Whereas the truth is that, reckoning in developmental time instead of clock-time, the creature that the midwife delivers from the maternal womb into the social womb is already wizened with age, and has arrived at the last few moments of its life as a condensation of Life.

Slower, less repressed, and much less spectacular is one's psycho-physical development, in the second or social womb, from the most vulnerable and handicapped of creatures into one capable (for example) of a triple salchow, of a break of 140 at snooker, of a *Times* crossword completed over breakfast, of a double first at Oxbridge. Or even (what's immeasurably more important and more difficult) capable of an honest and sustained acknowledgement of the superficiality of one's socialisation, of that secret and built-in selfishness and savagery that underlies its polished surface. And all this amazing expertise a condensation of five million years of human history and pre-history into a mere twenty years of life as the character who figures in one's birth-certificate and passport and identity-card!

Not bad, but certainly not enough. If you would like to see (repeat *see*) the Kingdom of God you must be born again.

You must see your way through from Womb 2 which is the human community into Womb 3 which is the spiritual community, the communion of those who distinguish who they *look like* at a distance of a metre or so from What they *are* at no distance, at Centre. The members of this spiritual community are scattered very thinly all over the world and talk the peculiar language of their respective religious traditions, but are nevertheless secretly and inwardly in constant touch with one another. It is, you might say, a very large womb, in which your embryonic and foetal development isn't less actual for being mostly hidden. Actual, and quite indispensable: for your first sighting of your True Identity, though impeccable, is very brief, and needs cultivating till it becomes steady and natural and effortless. Also your centre of gravity has to descend from head to heart and stay there. The love, the goodness, the beatific vision which the spiritual community have arrived at and enjoyed over the past four thousand years – all of this marvellous development is yours to arrive at and enjoy in as many days. Provided you want it enough.

Yours to arrive at and enjoy, but emphatically not to claim. Our third and ultimate birth – into God – confirms what has become increasingly evident: namely, the fact that such love and goodness and wisdom as we have, to say nothing of the beatific vision itself, is His and His alone. And yours and mine only insofar as we are by grace eternally united to Him.

Recapitulation, which is the condensation of history in successive wombs, is one of the great laws of life. And the ultimate condensation of history is in the Timeless One, the Eternal Being who is our Home.

(2) The Meaning-Shift

It is characteristic of development in a womb that it anticipates what will be needed after birth but is useless and meaningless now. What was the point of the hands you grew in your mother's womb where there was nothing to handle, of the lungs you grew where there was no air to breathe, of the eyes you grew in that thick darkness? They all came into their own and made sense when you were born into your second or social womb.

It is equally the case that the point and value of much of our human life in Womb 2 is revealed only at the next stage, in Womb 3.

Take eyes again, for instance. In Womb 2 we are sure we are looking at the world through our own *two* small peep-holes. It is only in our third womb that we come to our senses and start looking out of our immense single eye, which is the Eye of the one Seer in all beings. And here's a more personal example. The hidden reason for my early training in Womb 2 in graphic design, architecture, and structural engineering was its eventual application in Womb 3 to the structure and functioning of the First Person Singular. Thus the diagrams and charts, which are an essential part of my real job now, arise from skills acquired for quite another purpose in quite another world.

Moving on now from the particular to the general, the old cliché that this "vale of tears" is also a "vale of soul making" happens to be true. In our own language, if all human life and values and accomplishments end in decay and death and eternal oblivion, if that's all there is to them, they are in the last resort meaningless, and grinning Death the Reaper has the last laugh. Only by being born a third time, from Time into the Timeless, are Time's creatures, with all their agonies and ecstasies, so thoroughly *saved* that even the meanest of them is rendered meaningful and makes its indispensable contribution to the Total Picture.

"Whatever's that?" You ask.

Well, imagine a Rembrandt hanging in the National Gallery, and yourself a myopic fly strolling over its surface. You are unable to take in more than a tiny part of the whole at a time. The part of the picture that you have already walked over lies in the past, and the part you have still to walk over lies in the future. Meanwhile, what's present is this dark and dismal patch. But hope springs eternal in your insect breast. Behind you, in the past, were some colourful areas. Ahead of you, in the future, there may be others, just as bright and charming. Anyway at this point you are disturbed and take off, while still looking at the picture. And you discover that taking off from the picture is taking in more of the picture.

It is making *present* more and more of what you had either written off as past or put off as future. Till in the end – blessed fly! – you are more like one of God's angels enjoying His timeless-timeful masterpiece, which the Time-devil can hide but never destroy.

(And, dear angel, don't tell me that Eternity is eternally hidden from you. Your sort of angel wears a watch always, as well as B747 wings occasionally. Out there, in the time-world, your watch tells you the time, but you have only to bring it all the way up to your Single Eye to find it telling you the no-time right here. For here even the watch, let alone the figures and the hands, vanishes on close inspection. At Centre you are Eternity itself.)

PICTURE FRAME

To sum up, then, the successive meaning-shifts from one womb to the next are as follows. (a) From the useless organs of one's uterine life to their manifold uses in one's human life. (b) From the meaningless happenings of one's human life to their indispensable contribution to one's spiritual life. And (c) from the scattered adventures of one's spiritual life to their unification and completion in the Eternal Godhead.

(3) Delivery by Birth-Tunnel, or by Caesarean Section?

Your first birth, from the maternal womb into the social womb, was of course by one or other of these means. Either you were delivered in the usual way through the birth tunnel, or by surgical intervention.

Your second birth, from the social into the spiritual womb, is essentially similar. But this time the tunnel is a new-comer, and it's made of paper and not flesh and blood. And if I call it the *normal* mode of delivery (and I do) I certainly don't mean that it's the traditional way, or as yet at all common. What I do mean is that it has some striking advantages over what may be called the regular or "caesarean section" method of delivery, by which I mean any method which dispenses with a tunnel.

Your birth from the maternal womb into the social womb was once and for all. Not so your re-birth from the social womb into the spiritual womb. It's for constant repetition till you stay reborn. That's why I'm insisting that (no matter how often you have already done so) you make up a birth-tunnel now, consisting of two A4 sheets of paper stuck together along the short sides with sticky tape. And that you take it to your bathroom mirror, hold one end of the tunnel up against the glass, and fit your face in the other end. And that you actually undergo re-birth from Womb (2) where you are that obviously perishing human being, into Womb (3) where you are this obviously imperishable spiritual Being-NonBeing.

Never mind what you feel or think about the operation. It is enough that you take seriously what you *see* in the tunnel. To be re-born is to be the boundless, speckless, ageless, wide-awake Nothing-that-has-room-for-Everything, which is brilliantly on show at your end of it. In total contrast to that little old fellow at the far end.

In the social womb we don't see what we see, but what language and custom tell us to see. So that in all important respects we are the unconscious victims of mass hallucination. Particularly difficult to scotch is the basic delusion that one *is* here at Centre what one *looks like* over there. But get inside the paper tunnel, and at once the truth is inescapable: the total contrast between one's Reality at the near end and one's appearance at the far end couldn't be more obvious, more striking. Or more natural, more accessible at will, more shareable. Which must surely mean that our re-birth from Womb 2 into Womb 3 is no longer the privilege of a handful of gifted specialists, wearing very peculiar clothes and living very peculiar lives, but the norm for all of us ordinary folk who want to grow up.

To grow up, finally, into God, probably via our *third* birth-tunnel. (Yes, our God is indeed a *tunnelling* God!) Patients who have almost died, but have come back to tell their story, commonly speak of journeying along a dark and sometimes noisy tunnel towards a Light at the far end. And some have briefly joined that Light and found it to be indeed *the* Light, the welcoming but searching Light of God. But again there are many exceptions, and our final birth into Him may be by caesarean section, so to say, and via no tunnel. Let's see!

(4) Birth from Time into the Timeless

I think that the story of the fly that took off from the Rembrandt will help us here. Eventually (you'll remember) it distanced itself so far from the picture that it took in the whole of it. And it was no flawed or moth-eaten or fly-blown canvas that came to light. There were no useless surpluses or smudges in that all-inclusive masterpiece, to which even the tiniest and least interesting brush-mark made its indispensable contribution, no matter how and when the great painter laid it on, thick or thin, this way or that.

Which, being interpreted, means that every creature that is born into Time dies out of Time into the Timeless, into Eternity, where it will never die. Emily Bronte puts the matter with admirable clearness.

> *Though earth and man were gone,*
> *And suns and universes ceased to be,*
> *And Thou wert left alone,*
> *Every existence would exist in Thee.*
> *There is not room for Death,*
> *Nor atom that His might could render void:*
> *Thou – Thou art Being and Breath*
> *And what Thou art may never be destroyed.*

But will this do? You may well ask. What sort of afterlife is it – to be preserved for ever and ever in the cosmic deep-freeze, like a busy bee held fast in Eternity's amber? After all, it's the everlasting punishment of Lucifer, and by no means his salvation, that he's stuck head-first in the ice of Hell. I frequently describe myself –

this First Person Singular – as an Onion, each of whose skins comprises a regional appearance of the Reality at the Core. An encouraging and illuminating Self-portrait! But I would prefer extinction to eternal life as a *Pickled* Onion – if you could call it life at all. That sort of Birth into God at death would surely be worse than death.

It is also nonsense and pure fiction. The Picture that our fly takes off from and takes in is no static Old Master but a Movie, an Ever-changing, Ever-new Masterpiece, and as it changes so does the meaning, the role, the relevance of every part of it change. I guess it goes on and on being one jump ahead of itself. And that ultimately everything is everywhere at all times, as Whitehead used to say. Which means that the Universe will forever go on being different because you and I have as humans briefly happened in it, and our personal contribution will continue to mature endlessly. The mind boggles! Let it!

I conclude by wishing you the happiest of re-birthdays today – into the Birthless One. Here in Him and as Him your deepest and most contrasting needs are met. On the one hand you are born into everlasting Peace and Rest, into the Changeless, the Timeless, the incomparable and only Safety. And on the other hand into an ever-widening life of adventure and discovery, of newness, of surprises, of paradoxical birthday presents. You are born from Something into Nothing and Everything – Everything that is and was and shall be. You are born from Time into the Timeless and the Timeful that's always and never full. You are born from one who seems to be into the One who ISN'T and therefore IS *secula seculorum*, world without end, amen.

What more could you want? What less will do?

16

GOOD GOD –
BAD MAN

Valid spiritual principles aren't what they seem. Go into them,
start living from them, and they have a way of turning round, of
going into reverse. What at first seemed so negative and discouraging turns out to be nothing of the sort, and conversely what
seemed so positive and encouraging turns out to be, again, just the
opposite. Be prepared for surprises.

A striking instance of this turnabout is the Christian doctrine –
dismissed with contempt by the modern world, and ignored (if
not rejected) by many modern Christians – that man is intrinsically and by nature bad, and that any goodness he seems to have
isn't his at all but God's.

In fact this anti-humanist belief (some would go so far as to call it
anti-human) lies at the very heart of Christianity. From the start it
has been a vital part of the Faith. "Don't call me good," warns its
Founder, "only God is good." And St. Paul, self-confessed "chief of
sinners" and certainly chief fashioner of the Faith, writes to his
brethren in Rome, "I know that in me – that is in my flesh – dwells
no good thing." And this unflattering doctrine has held its own
throughout Christian history. Sometimes it has figured at the
forefront of consciousness, at other times lurked in the background.
Nevertheless, whether explicit or implicit, it was always there.

Always there, that is, till our time. Nowadays, with rare exceptions, the Christian as well as the non-Christian view is that the old idea of man's essential depravity – the notion that he's not only a bad lot but incapable of radical reform without divine intervention – is morbid and masochistic and very discouraging, a disincentive to virtue. If all our efforts to build a better world are flawed (if not futile) because they run counter to our nature, why bother? Why not give up the unequal struggle, and be the utterly selfish and unprincipled creatures that we are born to be? No wonder practically all of us nowadays are humanists of a sort, and our basic assumption is that – no matter how untapped and bunged up with every kind of rubbish – there exists in all of us an artesian well of human goodness. Draw on this well, and we behave humanely; fail to do so, and we behave inhumanely and often atrociously. It seems obvious that this view of our nature generates self-respect and may be counted on to bring out the best in that nature. Highly desirable goals which the outdated I'm-wickeder-than-you, self-denigrating piety rejected out of hand.

We must admit, I think, that at its own level this humanist attitude is both reasonable and practical. But there's another and higher level, a truer reason, a far more effective practicality. I'm convinced that Jesus and Paul got it right, and that the old good-God-bad-man doctrine, when understood and lived as it should be understood and lived and not merely theorised about, is what we deeply need and the radical answer to our otherwise desperate condition. In other words, it couldn't be more positive, more optimistic.

For of course there's a power of good in human beings. I find generosity and love and amazing self-sacrifice cropping up everywhere, not least in the most improbable places. The kindness of a passing stranger is sometimes enough to move one to tears. Yes indeed, but what makes this goodness so good is that it's in man but not of man. It is his by virtue of the fact that he's not only human, that in his depths lives the God (call Him or Her what you will) who is Goodness itself. Put it this way: the man who's not only man is a music in which the treble and the bass are as contrasting as they are complementary.

Or, to modernise the metaphor, he's a battery that's essentially bi-polar. Its twin electrodes carry opposite electric charges, and it is this, along with the distance between them, that generates the light in him. And the life in him, which (to the extent that it's lively) is a never-concluded argument between his two natures, a divine-human ding-dong. Anything he happens to do that's unselfish and beautiful, loving, inspired, and exceptionally well done, is done by the indwelling Divinity and not by (but rather, in spite of) that outdwelling human. The rest – and there's an awful lot of it – is that human's doing. All the same, both are needed. No polarity, no light.

But polarity doesn't mean parity. In every way the perfection of your divinity is prepotent: it has the edge on and transcends the innumerable imperfections of your humanity. A wise and kindly Providence has so fixed it that the good in you is more yours than the naughtiness is yours. And this is the way He works this miracle. The good you do is truly yours because it's done by the One you truly are, whereas the evil you do is done by the one you truly are not. Thanks to your most intimate union with Him in the depths, you are more Him and His deeds than you are you and your misdeeds. It's not that you deny and aren't bitterly sorry for those misdeeds (quite the contrary!) but that you deny their centrality. They are confessed, distanced, and forgiven. "Thy sins, saith the Lord, which were as scarlet, are as white as snow. Though they be red like crimson they shall be as white as wool."

Divine-human polarity brings many blessings in its train. One reason for the outstanding artistic and intellectual achievements of the ancient Greeks was that they had the modesty and good sense to attribute them to the Divine Muses rather than human cleverness. And one reason for the outstanding goodness of the man who said that only God is good was that he meant and lived what he said. Humanists can hardly pretend that they do better than him. It's time they stopped pretending they know better.

At this point I can hear you asking what proofs, what guarantees you have that all this talk of the Divine in us humans isn't wind and hot air, or at best a kind of imaginative poetry for cheering us up in a sad world.

The proof is to hand. All you have to do is to put aside your opinions and come to your senses and take a look at what's going on. Observe these printed words, these black marks on a white background. And observe what's 25cm nearer, what's right where you are right now, taking them in. Call it Aware Capacity or Conscious Accommodation or Space-for-those-things-to-happen-in. But never mind what you call it, notice that it's a boundless No-thing, empty for filling with any of those perishing things that are on offer (including the perisher in your mirror), but itself is imperishable. It is timeless and undying inasmuch as it is innocent of anything to register time with or to live and die. Notice also that it's the motionless container and observer of the movements of things. And above all notice that you are now wide-awake to Yourself as this and much more than this. You are, in fact, making the awesome discovery that whereas what you are looking at is secular, what you are looking out of is Divine. And you are also discovering that the Hindu and Sufi sages who said that God is the real Seer, that only He ever saw anything, were talking sense and knew what they were talking about.

But in the West, I can hear you responding, we tell a different tale. You challenge me to find a Christian saint or seer who would accept my sense-based proofs of the Immanent God, to say nothing of the unholy language they are couched in.

Well, let's see.

One of the most practical and saintly of my teachers is Jean Pierre de Caussade, S.J. (1675-1751). In a letter to one of his spiritual daughters he writes:

"Bear in mind the saying of St. François de Sales that you do not put on perfection as you put on a dress … Everything good in you originates in God, everything evil, spoilt, and corrupt originates in yourself. Set aside, then, negativity and sin, evil habits and inclinations, abysmal weaknesses and wretchedness. These are your portion, these originate in, and unquestionably belong, to you. Everything else – the body and its senses, the soul and its energies, the modicum of good that you have performed – are God's portion. It so manifestly belongs to Him that you realise you cannot claim a whit of it as yours, or feel one grain of complacency, without being guilty of theft and larceny against God."

Later on in the same letter, de Caussade describes the abyss of wretchedness into which we are thrust as "a supreme grace. For it is the basis of all distrust of self and of utter trust in God. These two are the poles of the interior life."

I would like to draw your attention to two things in these excerpts from de Caussade's letter.

1. He urges us to *set aside* our sin. Certainly not to deny it, but to deny its centrality in our life. We are to start living consciously from the other pole of our life, from our true Centre which is God Himself.

2. He ascribes the body *and its senses* to God and not to man. In effect he tells us, along with Zen Master Huang-Po, to rely on what we see and not on what we think. To which I would add: let's come to our senses, and they will take us Home to the God who alone makes perfect sense.

After all, then, the time-worn good-God-bad-Man set-up, which seemed so deplorably anti-humanist and even anti-human, turns full circle. Here at last is the true humanism: true because under-written by the One who (as de Caussade tirelessly points out elsewhere) goes to heart-rending lengths to prove that He, too, is Divine-Human, and as such essentially bi-polar.

17

THE SAMSON SOLUTION

This chapter falls into three parts – the Problem, the Parable, and the Solution suggested by the Parable.

The Problem, in a nutshell, is that I'm not as consistently happy as I think I should be. Just look at my good fortune! I couldn't see more clearly the Wonder that I am at Centre. I couldn't be more sure that This is the Highest, the Best, the Source, Reality Itself. I couldn't be more convinced of my union with This. Yet much of the time this tremendous realisation leaves me cold, or at least cool. Instead of finding myself in ecstasies I find myself for the most part in an off-white or light-grey if not sombre mood. Why?

Let me put the problem in traditional Indian terms. While *sat* (Being) and *chit* (Consciousness) are plentiful here, *ananda* (Bliss) is in comparatively short supply. But the scriptures amalgamate the three of them – *sat-chit-ananda* – in a kind of Holy Trinity, an indivisible Three-in-One. How is it, then, that I am not thrilled to the marrow, permanently overjoyed at my incredible and totally undeserved good fortune?

If you were kindly to ensure that this book becomes an all-time best-seller, or were to prescribe for me a medicine that would infallibly relieve me of all my aches and pains, or were to offer me your services as a jack of all trades or factotum for the rest of my life, just one of those mundane and comparatively trivial gifts would surely excite me more than all the *sat* and *chit* that are already mine in what should surely be Heaven on Earth. Why? Again, Why?

My guess is that you, dear fellow-seer, find yourself in the same boat. In a storm-tossed trimaran, two of whose hulls are seaworthy while the third is leaking, if in no danger of falling off. And my hope is that the following Parable will suggest how we can, nevertheless, together make harbour.

It's a very old story, and it comes from the Bible.

In all sorts of ways Samson was very special. An angel had appeared to his mother and foretold his conception. As he grew up the Spirit of the Lord came upon him so mightily that he became the hero and champion of the Israelites in their war against the Philistines. But in the end, through the treachery of his wife Delilah, they captured him, put out his eyes, and set him working at the prison mill with slaves. Then one day, at the great feast of their god Dagon, the lords of the Philistines had him brought to the temple where thousands were gathered, so that they could mock their erstwhile scourge and bitterest enemy.

Can you imagine a more desperate plight than poor Samson's? But he wasn't done for. His last exploit was his greatest victory over the Philistines. He caught hold of the twin pillars on which the whole superstructure of the temple rested, exerted his huge strength and pulled them in, thus bringing it all down on his persecutors, and, of course, on himself. Can you imagine a neater, more summary, swifter way out of his troubles? Or, for him personally, a more costly?

Now for the light which our story throws on our problem and its solution.

For a start, it suggests that I restate that problem in concrete, actual-factual terms, setting the present scene as vividly as that scene in Philistia some three thousand years ago.

Here am I, seated at this table, writing these words, in the living room of my house in Nacton, Suffolk, England. It's fairly well-built, and in no danger of early collapse. The walls are substantial and plumb-vertical. (If they were not, I, who architected and supervised

146

the construction of the building, would only have myself to blame.)

So far, so good. But my problem remains. Though nothing like so severe and dramatic as Samson's, it is essentially the same. We are both short of joy, because we are captive in Philistia. And by Philistia I mean the country where everything is amiss because it's founded on idolatrous fictions instead of the divinely given (and indeed obvious) truth. In fact my address, as recorded above, is incomplete. Like all countries on the map, England is a province of Philistia. This isn't the place to consider whether she could ever secede from that sinister Federation, but whether and how you and I can break free right now.

Samson – bless his broken heart – shows the way. *Let us pull in and pull down the walls of the room we happen to be sitting in.* With the help of this sketch I'll show you how I do it here, and you can then follow suit and do it where you are.

Shutting one eye and turning round as necessary, *I prolong downwards each vertical line that I see.* Using the edge of this book, or (better) a ruler or stick as indicated in the drawing, I prolong for instance the corners of the room, the door jambs, the upright members of the window frames, and so on. *And I find that all these supposedly vertical and parallel lines converge on me, coming together in the region of my heart.*

Now please repeat the experiment in the room you happen to be in at this moment.

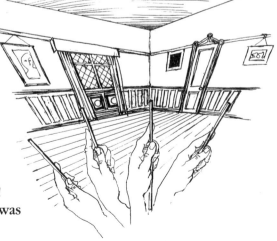

I don't know about you, but when I was at school they told me that parallel lines meet at Infinity. They were right! I am that Infinity! And so are you, and so was (or rather, is) Samson!

For check, let's point to this super-magnetic Centre that's pulling in every "vertical" line, and note that it's indeed infinitely deep, goes back and back for ever and ever.

We are starting to apply the Samson Solution to our troubles in Philistia, and it couldn't be more drastic, more deadly. Every one of those harmless verticals, those pillars of the temple, has become a lethal weapon. 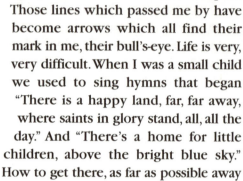 Those lines which passed me by have become arrows which all find their mark in me, their bull's-eye. Life is very, very difficult. When I was a small child we used to sing hymns that began "There is a happy land, far, far away, where saints in glory stand, all, all the day." And "There's a home for little children, above the bright blue sky." How to get there, as far as possible away from this "vale of tears", was not at all clear to us. But we had the right idea. What you might call our spiritual geography was sound. It's no good looking for Bliss down here. Bliss is an infinitely distant country, the other side of Death. And the reason why we aren't allowed in that blissful Heaven is that we fail to pay the very high price of admission, the price that Samson paid.

It isn't a price we pay once and for all. To confer its infinite blessing Death is a moment-by-moment, ever-renewed realisation. As for the *ananda*, the happiness that lights up that most distant yet nearest and dearest of countries (dearest in both senses), it is the steady climate of the place, built-in, forever absolutely perfect, and there's nothing that you and I have to do except submit to it and bathe in it.

I'll not try to describe what it feels like, except to say that it's the opposite of what passes for happiness in Philistia. You could call it a peace that's utterly devoid of excitement, but no description gets anywhere near the experience.

What to do, to enjoy this true happiness?

Death right now, which is really your ever-open door to eternal life, together with dear old Samson, and the leaning walls of the room you are sitting in at this very moment, plus your in-pointing finger, combine to give the answer: *Collapse! Fall away! Break down! Cave in! Fold up and up and up! Look in, and be reduced immediately to the Nothing that is Everything, and take what you get! It's all right!*

Postscript

Since writing this chapter, I have come across, in Dostoevsky's The *Brothers Karamazof* (trans. Pevear and Volkhonsky, Quartet Books, London, 1990), the following passage. Ivan Karamazov is speaking.

"There are philosophers who dare to dream that two parallel lines, which according to Euclid cannot possibly meet on earth, may perhaps meet somewhere in infinity ... I have a childlike conviction that the (world's) sufferings will be healed and smoothed over, that the whole offensive comedy of human contradictions will disappear like a pitiful mirage, a vile concoction of man's Euclidean mind ... And that, at the world's finale, there will be revealed something so precious that it will suffice for all hearts ... Let the parallel lines meet before my own eyes."

18

GORD
THE STORY OF
A LIFELONG
RELATIONSHIP

1

It began before I can remember. As I was born from the darkness of the womb into the air and the sunlight, so I was born into this most intimate personal relationship with Gord.

Yes, Gord was His name. I don't know why my father pronounced His name that way. It wasn't because he spoke broad Suffolk or broad North Essex. He didn't. Brethren from other parts of the country called Him Gord, too. Perhaps we all did so because Gord rhymes with Lord, which was His other name.

The Lord Gord was like a very special third granddaddy. My maternal granddaddy was short and had a dusty beard and was disagreeable; my paternal granddaddy was tall and had a white walrus moustache and was a darling; and my third granddaddy was gigantic and had a long snow-white beard and lived in Heaven above the bright blue sky and was disagreeable and a darling by turns, and sometimes both at once. You could describe our relationship as deep, but difficult and demanding on both sides.

The problem was not that, unlike the other two, He was so far off. Quite the contrary. It was rather that He was so close, with us all the time. Not, of course, as an ordinary member of the family

but as its undisputed Boss, its invisible and therefore exceptionally intrusive and nosy Overseer. Though His home address was
Heaven, ours was His home-from-home, all right. There was no
getting away from Gord. Every night we children talked to Him on
our knees before jumping into bed. Every morning and evening
my father talked to Him at length while we all knelt and were
expected to listen and keep our eyes closed and not to fidget. Also
my father had a short talk with Him before and after each meal.

You might think that this added up to enough Gord-talk per
day. But not so. Every day except Sunday father read to us a
different chapter of the Book that Gord has written. A few of the
chapters were exciting and rough-and-tumble or even gory, but
most were dreadfully dull. Listening to father's embarrassment
when he came to the rude parts of the Book afforded occasional
light relief, as did his pathetic attempts to pronounce the names in
those chapters that consist of names and very little else. What
made those tongue-twisters worth the effort was (I gathered) the
fact that Gord had written them in His Holy Book, which was
enough to make them holy too.

In addition to this intensive daily routine, we had Gord in a
very special way on Sundays. At least the grown-ups did. They ate
bits of Him and sipped His blood (or so they said), and my father
was invariably on the verge of tears as He went on about the
incredible love which the meal was all about. All this, along with a
lot of other remarkable things that went with it, I took on board
without questioning or understanding a word of it. That wasn't
what it was for. I felt it, absorbed it by virtue of a kind of osmosis.
Inevitably, in one guise or another, it got incorporated, became an
essential part of what I am to this day.

I'm not complaining. In what I've just said I've made Him sound
too pushy and very demanding. But there really was something
marvellous, though utterly mysterious and indescribable, about my
heavenly granddaddy, Something that warmed me up inside and
made me want to breathe deeply and run as fast as I could and
smile a secret sort of smile. It was as if He were my Sun and my
sunlight. I even found myself loving Him a lot, at times, and falling
back into the safety of His great arms.

152

The practical problem was that He turned out so often to be on the side of my mother. In league with her against me, for example, in such matters as reading the Bible, and table manners, and being seen but not heard, and no games whatever on Sundays. And of course, because about half the things I wanted to do upset her, they had to upset Him also. For, in spite of this unusual introduction to life, I was on the whole a normal sort of boy. Which is to say naughty, and sometimes very naughty. Indeed wicked in the eyes of my mother (and Gord, of course), and in danger of Hell. The Lord Gord's Second Coming was long overdue, and could happen at any moment. Then all His friends, the good and saved people, would join Him in the sky and go up to Heaven, while all His enemies, the bad and lost ones (including me) would be left on earth and go down to Hell and be burned alive for ever and ever and ever. And sure enough one day, arriving home early from school, I couldn't find my parents. Nowhere was there any trace of them. "They've been caught up with the Lord to Heaven, and here am I left down here and going to Hell for ever," was my instant reaction. More than eighty years later I can remember my terror. Those eternal flames! Were they any less agonising because they were (according to my dear father) the form that separation from Him happened to take down there. Wilful separation.

Such - for better rather than for worse, I would say - was my childhood relationship with Him, its foundation. But of course as the child grew up so did the relationship. At seventeen I managed to persuade myself that I was "saved", and I started participating in those Lord's-day meals reserved for His people. But before long my salvation turned out to be woefully deficient, I began to suffer increasingly from a double failure: failure to believe all I was told about Gord, and failure to do all I was told to do by Him. Doubt and guilt, and the doubt helped me to cope with the guilt.

The tension built up, Something had to give.

2

It did. At twenty-one I apostatised from the Brethren and became - not an unbeliever or even an agnostic, but what might be called a half-hearted gnostic. Both He and I, entering the second phase of our relationship, underwent a drastic sea-change. My leaving home and going to the university (and, incidentally, going to the theatre and cinema for the first time) made a huge difference to me, while His change of name from Gord to Atman Brahman Buddha Tao God Allah, along with His change of role from granddaddy to distant relation, made a huge difference to Him. From then on, as befits distant relations, we exchanged Christmas cards, so to say, and certainly I never quite forgot Him any more than He forgot me. It was as if He'd been vaporised and distributed but by no means abolished.

Accompanying the process of de-materialising Him went the contrary process of solidifying and individuating me, with the result that we drifted further and further apart. No longer was He the kind of person you talk to or unload your troubles on. I got the idea that I could manage pretty well without Him, thank you very much. He came to resemble a rather nebulous uncle in Australia who, because he might one day leave me a fortune, deserved to be kept in touch with.

But of course it didn't quite turn out that way.

3

Whether because of the misery and loneliness of life without Him, or the inexorable pull of my childhood attachment to Him, or His grace and loving kindness, at the age of thirty-two I was suddenly impelled to seek Him in all earnestness. Not, this time, in the Heaven above the bright blue sky, or in meeting rooms or monasteries or temples or churches, but in my heart, my inmost being. For it was here that the sages I most respected – whatever tradition they happened to belong to – advised me to look for Him. Moreover the possibility that His home should be nearer to me than my home, or should indeed be my true and eternal home, appealed to me strongly.

So I looked in my heart for Him. And at once, without the slightest difficulty or delay, I found Him. He had been patiently waiting here all the while, at my very centre, begging to be noticed. Eagerly He showed Himself to me as ultra-obvious, immense, immaculate, all-inclusive, unborn, undying, unmoving, and wide-awake to Himself, as all this and much more, beyond all doubting. I saw Him far more clearly than anything else, as Clearness itself. He was in, Harding was out. He was my Sun and my sunlight, my King, my cure, my largeness, my life, my me. Or rather, more me than me. He gave Himself to me completely, in such a way that I could never lose Him.

What I had to do now was three things. To keep coming back to this many-sided but perfectly simple vision of Him in me and as me till it became constant, to hand over to Him the running of my life in general and in detail, and to share with a blind and suffering world the Eye-opener He had entrusted me with.

A full programme, for sure! Impossible of full attainment it would seem, and certainly more than enough to keep me busy for this, the third (and by far the longest) phase of my relationship with Him.

To what extent can I report success?

Well, slowly but surely, I moved in. After a few years of practice I ceased to live an eccentric life looking in at my superficial self, and started to live a centred life looking out from my deepest self, which is none other than Him. Proof that this shift had actually happened was the surprising fact that I no longer felt under people's inspection. It seemed that along with Him I had taken on His invisibility. An immense relief and advantage! Further confirmation of the shift came from the equally surprising fact that I found myself looking through His own immense Single Eye at the world (ranging from telegraph poles to mountains and stars and galaxies) that He sets in motion from His (and my) stillness. So far, so good.

Far less successful was my ever-renewed attempt to shift from my will to His. Shades of the old old trouble: He was still so often "on the side of my mother". Sure enough, the shift came to be not too difficult in little things, such as saying Yes to a bout of indigestion, or moles in the garden, or a huge bill from the plumber. But very difficult indeed in big things, such as saying Yes to the multiple and ever-growing handicaps that go with being an ageing human being. Here I have to report dismal and near-total failure. Also failure to feel as bright and bushy-tailed as I think I should feel, seeing that I have for Guest this much-more-than-Guest and for Friend this much-more-than-Friend.

As for my lifelong attempt to share the great vision with others, to devise ways of demonstrating the marvel that they are, to interest them in themselves – let alone Him – I have again to report much failure. Any success has been due to my giving up any idea of success and handing the work over to Him whose work succeeds in His own time and His own way.

And so it goes. Life with Him at my centre is radically different from life with Him way over there, and for sure from life without Him. It's a life bursting with meaning, you could say, though by no means problem-free. You could sum it up as an endlessly repeated exercise in coming back from me there to Him here, from me as me who am nothing to me as Him who is All.

It has been enough to keep me busy for the past half-century or so. Nevertheless, to my surprise and perhaps yours, this is by no means the end of my story. There's an all-important sequel. My relationship with Him enters its fourth phase. A phase which overlaps the third by a long way, while contrasting with it sharply.

4

The startling thing about this phase of the spiritual adventure is that it reads like a defeat, the loss of all the hard-won gains of those long years of spiritual endeavour. To call it a disappointment is a monumental understatement. I have to face the fact that the goal of "union with Him at my centre" won't do, quite apart from the question of whether it's attainable or not. So what's missing? What could I lack if I have Him?

Actually the trouble is plain to see. The three words "I have Him" say it all. They give the game away. What I have been doing all along is to chase Him as if He were the rarest and most gorgeous of butterflies, with a view to netting Him, pinning Him down, and putting Him on display at the head of my spiritual collection. How's that for presumption?

Not that I had any option. This hot pursuit has been my proper business all through the third (and indispensable) phase of my relationship with Him. And His proper business all through has been to get away, which of course He always does. And no wonder! All right, I do have Him at my centre: but I must point out that this centre explodes, on inspection, to infinity, so that He has all the room He needs to escape in. The truth is that He's for chasing always, catching never.

That's why St John of the Cross warns us: "Never forget that God is inaccessible. Ask not therefore how your powers may comprehend Him. Fear thus to content yourself with too little, and deprive yourself of the agility which you need in order to mount up to Him." (Butterfly hunters need to be nimble.) Elsewhere St. John elaborates the paradox: "One of the greatest favours bestowed on the soul transiently in this life is to enable it to see so distinctly and to feel so profoundly that it cannot comprehend God at all. These souls are herein somewhat like the saints in Heaven, where they who know Him most perfectly perceive most clearly that He is infinitely incomprehensible: for those who have the less clear vision do not perceive Him so clearly as do those others how greatly He transcends their vision."

Other masters have the same message. For instance, Eckhart: "The more God is in all things the more He is outside them."

How can you and I guard against all efforts to tame and domesticate Him, to weigh Him up and come to terms with Him?

I know of only three ways. First, never forget that He's the Self-Originator, that He has the "impossible" knack of Being-from NonBeing, of inventing Himself; and, along with Himself, everything else, including you and me. Domesticate *that* – if you can! The second way to let the Butterfly God go is to see that you have no butterfly net, no container here to contain anything, let alone Him. And the third way is to remember that, in truth, only He ascends to the All because only He sinks to the Nothing. When we deny ourselves humanly it's in order to promote ourselves spiritually: we go down in order to go up, whereas He goes down in order to go down. He alone is great enough to be so humble on our behalf. Which is another aspect of that "impossible" knack of His.

Well, it has been a funny-peculiar but most intimate relationship with Gord, alias God.

He began as a bossy but adorable granddaddy for talking to, went on to become a vast interior ocean for exploring and bathing in, and ended as a gorgeous butterfly or will-o'-the-wisp for chasing unsuccessfully.

Once again I'm not complaining. Taking my cue from the man who said that a club that would have him wouldn't be worth belonging to, I say that a Deity that I could apprehend and comprehend wouldn't be worth the bother. Yet my need of Him is such that I have to have Him. How do I have Him? As the One that always escapes me. But not before He whispers in my ear, "And that's the way that I – I who am built in your image as surely as you are built in Mine – have Myself."

19

BATH-HOUSE PAINTINGS

You see them looking but they are like paintings
in a bath-house:
they do not see. The form appears, O worshipper of form,
as though those two dead eyes were looking.
Jalalu'ddin Rumi

By "paintings in a bath-house" Rumi means graffiti, not proper and approved decorations. For representation of the human form was forbidden in Islam because it was reckoned likely to lead from worship of the One God to the worship of many gods, to all sorts of idolatry. That is why mosques and tombs are to this day decorated with arabesques, or patterns derived from plants, or abstract forms.

The question this chapter addresses is: Was the great Rumi right to insist on two things – first, that eyes don't see; and second, that it's important to realise and see that they don't see, to despook them, so to say. Do we in fact need to exorcise the sprites that haunt or seem to haunt not only pictures and sculptures of people, not only our own reflections in mirrors, but also the eyes and faces of all the people we meet? If so, how should we go about this necessary but difficult business of wholesale exorcism?

159

But is it necessary? You may well ask. Was it perhaps a quirk or whimsical flight of Rumi the poet rather than a warning of Rumi the sage? No! Other Sufis were equally sure of it, and some were even more sweeping. Take for example Bayazid of Bistun: "I looked and saw that all created things are dead. I pronounced four akbirs over them and returned from the funeral of them all. And, without intrusion of creatures, through God's help alone, I attained unto God."

Nor is this basilisk-like attitude to our fellow human beings confined to Muslims who are so anxious to guard against idolatry. Zen Buddhism tells us: "Only when you find no things in consciousness, and no consciousness in things, are you empty and spiritual, formless and marvellous." (Po-shan) And "Where others dwell I do not dwell, where others go I do not go. This doesn't mean that I refuse to associate with other people, but that black and white must be distinguished" (Pai-yun). As for Christianity, St Paul regards his Colossian disciples as dead, and their life as hidden with Christ in God. All very different in style and vocabulary from Rumi, of course, but the same in substance and purpose. And there are loud echoes, as we shall presently see, in Advaita-Vedanta, couched, again, in its own vernacular. Now when the great spiritual traditions are agreed on something, no matter how strange or difficult that something may seem, and go to much trouble to rub it in, be sure that we pooh-pooh that something at our peril.

This is all the more true when it also crops up strongly in our own spiritual tests or exercises or experiments, for example in our Tunnel Experiment.

This is how you carry out the Tunnel experiment, and to get the point of it it's no good just reading about it. You have to do what I say.

Make a paper tube about six inches in diameter and about ten inches long. Fit your face into one end of it and hold the other up against your bathroom mirror. And observe how what's seen, all the stuff in the tube, has gravitated to the far end; and how what sees, all the consciousness in the tube, has gravitated to the near end, to your end of the tube.

Here's a double de-contamination: that end is cleansed of phantoms and sprites and consciousness in general, while this end is cleansed of matter and stuff of any kind.

Now repeat the experiment with a friend's face at the far end of the tube instead of yours – with similar results?

Are those findings any different outside the tube? I suggest that you need the tube no longer in order to see what the great seers saw. Namely that Awareness belongs only to the Subject – which in the last resort is none other than the Indivisible and Suprapersonal Subject that you and I really are – and never to its object as such.

To check that this is so, just look and make sure that the Clarity you are now looking out of at this printing is big enough, and awake enough, and impersonal enough, to serve as the inside story of all beings, none of whom can claim it as their personal property.

Now it seems to me that when we are carrying out this Tunnel Experiment, and more importantly when we are living as best we can in the light of what we learn fom it, we are in danger of neglecting what's given there in the object, in favour of what's given here in the Subject. We are better at unthinging this subject here than at unspooking that object there. We hedge our bets, we compromise. Not all the consciousness in our world is collected in this Consciousness right here and right now. Enough of it is left out there to haunt somewhat the faces and eyes that confront us. In a word, we remain idolaters, polytheists in some degree.

The consequences of our uneasy compromise are twofold.

First, we remain self-conscious instead of Self-conscious. In company we still tend to feel under inspection, unable to gaze comfortably into those seemingly critical eyes, and this inhibits the spontaneous and free-flowing behaviour that each unique occasion calls for. Situations crop up when we are awkward and unnatural. While it may be true that our practice of facelessness has cured us largely of shame-facedness, remnants of it will go on troubling us till we cease attributing sight to eyes.

The second consequence of our partial failure to profit by and follow through to the end the discoveries that we made in the tube, is that the One Consciousness at this end of it is reduced to less than itself. Less by all those little consciousnesses that we robbed the One of so casually and handed out so freely to the Many. With the inevitable result that we lack confidence in the One that's One no longer, in our now-denuded Source and Resource. How can I abandon the whole of myself to one who's not quite whole, or enjoy perfect union with one who isn't perfectly unified, who isn't quite all there (as we say), or be healed by one who can do with a spot of healing?

The combined result of these two lapses of attention is that we cut God down to less than God and build His creatures up to more than creatures, which is to inject large doses of devilry into them. For let's face it, consciousnesses split off from their Divine Source don't stay divine. Quite the contrary! I'm reminded of a grievous problem I had when I was a little boy. I was made to use a bowl at the bottom of which were inscribed the words *Thou God Seest Me* and a great staring EYE. How reluctant I was to finish my porridge and expose that diabolical thing!

Attributing sight to eyes isn't only idolatrous and handicapping and scary. It's unscientific.

In summary, science's story of how I see you is an eightfold cosmic process, an eight-step hierarchical descent, like this: Light rays from our Galaxy (1), in particular from our Sun (2), after filtration by Earth's atmosphere (3), bounce off you (4), and form two upside-down pictures of you on the screen at the back of my eyeballs. The resulting changes in the light-sensitive cells (5) of which the screen is composed are passed on to the molecules (6) of the chemical substance (rhodopsin) in which those cells are embedded. These changes are conveyed along the optic nerves to a special region of the brain whose atoms (7) and particles (8) take up the story. Beyond these, shrouded in absolute mystery, lies the Terminus. *It's not till this Terminus is reached that I see you.*

So much for science's account of how I see you. Let me now translate it into the language of this book.

Only God sees. Only the God who is at once No-thing at the base and centre of His cosmic hierarchy, and All-things at its peak and circumference, actually sees any of those things. Seeing is His job. Attributing it to eyes and to the people that are eyeing you, is a superstition way behind the scientific times. It is also attaching yourself to people by bonds of liking and disliking, of anxiety and fear, of dependence and the need to dominate, and so on and on. Conversely, ceasing to attribute sight to them is to break those bonds and arrive at the non-attachment that the sages speak so highly of.

The Taoist sage Chuang-Tzu comes up here with the perfect metaphor. Suppose you are at sea in a small boat, and another small boat is about to collide with you. Furious with its careless skipper, you rain down curses on him. But if the boat is empty you stay cool. And then if you are sensible (let me add) you take that empty boat in tow as your prize.

But here we run into difficulties. "What about love?" we ask. What about the attachment that refuses to reduce the loved one to a ship without a sailor, to a cardboard cut-out? What's wrong with that refusal, for God's sake, and what's right without it? In fact here, on the face of it, is a major contradiction that's built in to the great spiritual traditions. Take the following instances.

"Though I speak with the tongues of men and of angels," says St Paul, "and have not love, I am become as sounding brass and tinkling cymbal." And the Sermon on the Mount, delivered by Paul's Lord and Master, was indeed a superb plea for unconditional love, love for your neighbour, for your enemy, for your persecutor. Yet how soon that sermon was followed by the warning: "If any man come to me and hate not his father, and mother, and wife, and children, and brethren, and sisters … he cannot be my disciple." And many of his disciples have heeded that warning with a vengeance. The Blessed

Angela of Foligno, for instance, though a gifted mystic, announced quite cheerfully: "At that time by God's will there died my mother, who was a great hindrance to me in following the Way of God. Soon also died my husband likewise, and also my children. And because I had commenced to follow the aforesaid Way, and had prayed to God that He would rid me of them, I had great consolation of their deaths." Even so moderate and humane a spiritual director as Jean-Pierre de Caussade writes to one of his flock: "Let me in all sincerity disclose a fear I have on the subject of yourself. In my opinion your too-frequent contact with your many relatives and others in the world are a stumbling-block to your advancement ... You know how this snare threatened disaster to St Teresa."

Evidently we have here a serious dilemma, a practical problem that cries out for resolution. Nor is it a problem for individuals only. To see how far-reaching and deep its social consequences can be, take India and Hinduism. The ancient sages of the Upanishads made the awesome discovery that only God sees, and that He is Who one really is, the Alone. As for the others, there are no others! And, insofar as they do exist, their misfortunes are the inevitable result of their ignorance and bad behaviour in past lives, their negative karma. Now it's hardly surprising that this wisdom has made for indifference to the plight of India's poor and sick. So we ask: what went wrong, what's missing from the wisdom that turned out to be so socially insensitive, so uncaring, so unwise?

There is a resolution to our problem, and it runs like this.

To quote Jesus Christ himself again: "Know the truth, and the truth shall set you free." And the truth in this instance is that whereas all the eyes you ever saw are blind, none of their owners are blind. All see with the One Eye of the One Who Sees. Again, the truth is that while all creatures are in themselves dead, in the timeless God they live forever. He is in them as their consciousness, their being, their life. And that ruthless reduction of your neighbour to less than a bath-house painting, along with that cheerful polishing-off altogether of your nearest and dearest – what is it, after all? It is your point-blank refusal to stop short of that Divine Centre where we are all reduced to Nothing whatever. Thereby becoming one with the One Who is All, the One Who is Love indeed.

20

MR SMITH GOES TO HEAVEN

Mr. Smith dies and goes to Heaven, where he humbly begs a favour of St Peter. He would be very grateful if an early interview with the Lord God could be arranged.

His request is granted. Here is the conversation which followed.

Mr. Smith I have been a lifelong believer, a loyal and devoted subject of your Divine Majesty.

Lord God Thank you, Mr. Smith.

MS I have often thought how wonderful it must be to be You.

LG Yes indeed. I am quite bowled over with astonishment.

MS Just fancy being the Being that has to be, the necessary Backing that's at the back of everything! The Launch-pad that must be in place before any of us can take off into existence!

LG You say I have to be. Please explain, Mr. Smith.

MS Well, if anything's a Dead Cert (as we say on Earth), a *fait accompli*, the Bottom Line, our Sure Foundation – why, it's You, Lord, who are Being Itself.

LG Do you mean that I'm inevitable, the one indispensable Foregone Conclusion? That until I'm taken for granted nothing's granted?

MS Precisely, Your Majesty. Being has to be.

LG I have to say that I don't quite recognise Myself in this description, Mr. Smith.

MS But You are the One who holds the key to the deepest basement of the world, who ensures the everlasting safety and solidity and certainty of the Rock of Being on which You build the towering structure of Your Universe.

LG I'm sorry to disappoint you, Mr. Smith, but I hold no such key. In fact I'm unsure of the foundation which you say I ensure.

MS What! This is awful! Don't tell me that You, who are Being Itself, are wobbly, uncertain of Your ground, ignorant of Your origin and *raison d'être*!

LG There's no need to get upset. I don't think there's much risk of Being grinding to a halt, or of your Rock starting to rock, or of my own early demise. However, Mr. Smith, that doesn't mean that I have to be, any more than you have to be.

MS I'm dumbfounded.

LG So am I. And the reason why my coming-to-be leaves me clueless and dumbfounded is quite simple. It is this. To get cracking, to make myself happen, to initiate and supervise my own emergence and waking from the long night of nothingness, I would have to be in place before there was any place to be in, around in advance of myself, there before I was there, present while I was as yet absent. Which is a contortion that even I am incapable of – thank goodness.

MS And I had believed that you were all-powerful and all-knowing! Such impotence and ignorance at the very top (or do I mean at the very bottom?) must sadden and humiliate you. Not to mention the risk you run of being charged with false pretences by your own...

LG Go on, Mr. Smith.

MS I'm utterly baffled. I hardly know whether to be frightened of you, or bitterly disappointed with you, or sorry for you.

LG Your pity at least, Mr, Smith, is misplaced. I love being the way I am. I'm thrilled and wonder-struck to be the Great Improbable. *Correction:* the Great Impossible, to be which is a very special kind of joy. And I can't think of any state more joyless, more deadly dull, more dead than your "dead-cert" Being, your has-to-be Being. I would hate to be the Being that could take snapshots of itself from every angle, that had got itself neatly taped, that had itself for breakfast and lunch and dinner. No mystery, no magic, no marvel, no miracle at the beating heart of the world – now there's heartbreak, there's cardiac arrest for you! Spare your pity, Mr. Smith, for *that* patient!

MS There's one thing that has to be, and that's Being. I believe in the Rock of Ages that none of your atheistic dynamite could tickle, let alone blow sky-high. And I certainly don't believe in an atheist God who seems so eager to light the fuse.

LG Bear with me a little longer, Mr. Smith, while I explain. Really there should be nothing at all, no consciousness, no Lord God, no Mr. Smith, not so much as a sand-grain or a sigh. Their coming to be, my own coming from nowhere and nowhen, is shockingly but delightfully *unnatural*, against all conceivable odds. Yet it happens, and with what ease and panache, what thrust, what vigour! This crown of mine (undeserved in your opinion) has probably prevented you from noticing how my hair stands permanently on end with wonder and gratitude (to whom?) for my own arrival on the scene, thanks to no outside help and for no reason whatever.

MS Then who are you? I nearly said: who the devil are you?

LG Good question. You could call me the Being-that-shouldn't-be. Or, as I much prefer, the God who is not God, the Someone who's No-one – in sharp contrast to the pseudo-God who's only God, to the toffee-nosed Being who never deigns to come down from his pedestal and splash about in the clear water of NonBeing at its base.

MS Are you seriously asking me to believe in a God who doesn't believe in himself, who's incapable of living up to his own Godhood? Do you expect me to bow before a crippled Deity, one that suffers from a fatal flaw?

LG What you read as a flaw, as feebleness and failure, I read as FLAIR, as the Wonder that makes everything wonderful. When, on the other hand, you set up an all-round-knowable, tidy, self-consistent, manageable Something as the Source of everything, a vital ingredient is missing from all it produces – a morning freshness, a fire and a freedom, a radiance and a music and a perfume. The only smell it gives off is the stale body-odour of that heavily brooding and unremarkable Source. I say: only discover, back of yourself and all things, the lightsome and utterly transparent Nothing from which they are forever arising, and then you have that vital ingredient in full measure. The truth is that this factory called Nothing not only produces and markets everything wholesale, but fortifies the least of its retail merchandise with its own special quality. I'm inviting you, Mr. Smith, to share my astonishment and the joy of it.

MS You've got quite a thing about this Nothing, haven't you? Well, I haven't. For me Nothing is nothing, a write-off, a dead loss, a bore, a great big y-a-w-n.

LG Hold on, Mr. Smith! I admit I took off just now and let myself go a bit. Let's get down to the practical details of life. When you see or hear anyone, when you take in any scene, sensation, idea – anything whatever – you make way for it, you entertain it and give it house-room. Its thingness unthings you. Its presence is your absence. And why? Because you are built like that. Well, so am I. Truly, truly, Mr. Smith, I am empty for filling with you at this moment. I die that you may live. I sink into No-Godness so that you may rise into Smithness. No Nothing, no thing. All the somethings of our life are so many ships afloat on the shoreless Ocean of Nothingness. How's that for buoyancy? But I'm forgetting that Captain Smith is currently in dry dock.

MS At the beginning of this interview you failed to recognise yourself in my portrait of you. Well, here's my *quid pro quo*: I certainly don't recognise myself in your portrait of me. I reject this obsession with Nothing. Why? Because it's morbid, it's life-denying, it's masochistic, it's even a kind of attempted suicide.

LG That's because you mistake conscious Nothingness for unconscious annihilation, for the end of you instead of the ever-renewed beginning, and are naturally terrified. If you were to pick up your courage and say a hearty YES to it you would realise that it is the medicine for your fear of death, and for death itself. You would find in it your coming to be instead of your coming to pass. You might even go on to discover that it's the Light that lights up the light, the highest that's the highest only because it's also the lowest, the leaven in the Bread of Life and the alcohol in the Wine of Life, the Secret Weapon in the holy war against all wickedness and ugliness and lies. One thing's for sure: you would not find it dull or tame. It's things that are dull and tame, apart from their Primary Producer. When, in the cool of the day, I walk with Adam in the garden, it really is a walk on the wild side. Shall we take a little stroll together, Mr. Smith?

MS (*backing away from the throne*) There's been a dreadful mix-up. What shall I do?

LG You will find a busy shuttle service between here and that Other Place. It will take you to the Stately Home of the Stately Somebody who's determined not to let himself down by becoming Nobody, or disappearing in anyone's favour. So it's not *adieu*, Mr. Smith, but *adiable*. Or may I say *au revoir*?

Exit Mr Smith, muttering.

21

CHIAO'S DREAM

Here, form is emptiness and emptiness is form.
Here is no eye, no ear, no nose, no tongue.
Here is no birth or decay or death.
Therefore the Bodhisattva ceases to tremble,
For what could go wrong?
Gone, gone beyond, gone to the other shore!
Condensed from the Heart Sutra

Chiao allowed himself a broad, satisfied smile.

"Today," he announced to his fellow monks, "is a red-letter day for me. I have just made my ten-thousandth recitation of the precious Heart Sutra, which of course is the quintessence of the Mahayana and of the teaching of the Blessed One."

After everyone else had offered his respectful congratulations, the novice Tsung approached Chiao and, with many bows, asked if the meaning of the Sutra could be explained to him.

So taken aback by this strange request was Chiao that he found himself quite at a loss for words. But after a long silence he replied: "It is an extremely ancient and holy and powerful scripture. So much so that reciting it with the correct postures for many years must have beneficial effects, which for the most part are hidden.

As for any merit that may accrue, I dedicate it to all sentient beings. But surely, though a beginner, you must know that this Scripture is so sacred and so profound that it is recited daily in all Mahayana monasteries."

"I gather, reverend sir," replied the young novice, renewing his bows, " that the Sutra is so holy that it's for reciting, and by no means for understanding."

"The floor of the meditation hall badly needs sweeping," Chiao retorted. He was upset, and all the more because he was not very clear why. Upset, in part, because he had allowed a mere novice to spoil what had promised to be a very special and happy day.

That night he had a dream.

There appeared before him the towering, golden form of the Buddha, radiating beams of light and smiling compassionately. "What can I do for you?" he inquired, in a voice that was pure music.

"Ten thousand times, O Holy One, I have recited your precious words announcing that form is emptiness. Ten thousand times! But the forms that this despicable monk comes across are full. Bark encloses solid timber, right to the heart of the tree. Broken stones turn out to be stone all through. Wounded men are plainly made of flesh and blood. Even empty pots are brim-full of air."

"I understand your problem perfectly," replied the Buddha. "and here's what I will be happy to do to help you. I'll fix you up with your very own specimen form that is plainly empty. You could then take that specimen as a true sample of the forms that appear to be full, as their inside story, so to speak. Would you like that?"

"I would be eternally grateful to the Holy One."

"No sooner said than done! You are from now on equipped with your very own parcel of the Form-that-is-void. What's more, you shall have it always to hand, ready for instant inspection. You will always be able to see, with perfect clarity, its perfect emptiness."

"My gratitude is boundless," replied Chiao. "But ..." he hesitated, "if it's *that* empty how shall I know it is there at all? Won't it be quite undetectable?"

"Your difficulty has been forestalled. You will have plenty of clues as to the Form's presence, clues that nevertheless will not in the slightest degree cloud its transparency. You will, for instance, be able to touch it. In fact, to finger the thing all over to your heart's content."

"I was just wondering," replied the monk very nervously, "whether this amazing combination of invisibility and tangibility might be a bit awkward sometimes. Won't I keep bumping into the thing? Forgive these stupid questions, Holy One!"

"Not stupid at all! I have already arranged for it to follow you around like the most devoted and self-effacing of servants. In fact to be physically attached to you. You will always find it within easy reach, yet sufficiently out of the way wherever you go – except, perhaps, through low doorways."

"Praise to the Exalted One! A many-faceted miracle indeed! Never mind if I look slightly ridiculous, going round with my special lump of Nothingness, and fingering it from time to time to see if it's still there. Rather like a worried Egyptian scarab with its precious ball of dung."

"In the country of lunatics the sane man *is* ridiculous. But not to worry. People will never notice. Is there anything else I can do for you on this red-letter day?"

"Well I was just wondering about this. In the sacred Sutra you not only teach that form is void but also that the void is form. But how can my sample Emptiness be or contain anything without ceasing to be empty? This stupid monk is bewildered."

"Only give it a trial, Chiao, and you'll find it all makes good sense. Just now it may sound to you quite impossible, but I promise that you will be able clearly to see that your own absolutely speckless Void contains innumerable forms. Or rather that it *is* those forms, which are infinite in number and scope and variety. Your own personal parcel of emptiness, though small enough for you to handle all over, will be visibly packed full with the blazingly colourful, gigantic, rip-roaring world. And therefore as big, if not bigger, than that world."

"I can't thank the Holy One enough for these quite impossible miracles. Added to which is the equally impossible miracle that here (as you go on to say in the Holy Sutra) are no eye, no ear, no tongue, no nose. I, for one, live under the illusion that I have them here, more or less in good working order."

"I have already arranged for their instant amputation," replied the Buddha, quite casually.

"Oh dear!" gasped Chiao.

"Quite painlessly, of course," added the Buddha, soothingly. "And what's more, I think you will find that your eyesight and hearing and tasting and smelling will be all the keener for this surgery."

"The Compassionate One has already bestowed on this unworthy monk too many wonderful gifts. But there remains one very serious difficulty. The Holy Sutra denies that there is any decay or death. But I notice, with more alarm than surprise, that I'm made of very perishable stuff indeed."

"The matter has already been attended to. It's up to you from now on to see that in truth you consist of a quite marvellous substance that can never change. And by *you* I mean what's right where you are right now, what you are coming from. Clean of all distinguishing characteristics, it manifestly can never suffer the slightest injury or deterioration, much less perish."

"Forgive me, O Holy One, for doubting whether I could begin to live this astounding new life here on the stormy shore of Samsara, with all its illusion and pain and squalor, so very far from the further shore of Nirvana. Alas, I'm assured that the voyage to that blessed haven is long and dangerous and difficult, and (all those prostrations notwithstanding) impossible for me in this life, unless … unless …"

The Buddha smiled. "All right," he said in a voice that was purest compassion, "you are across! Gone, gone, gone right over! Or rather, come, come right over. You are established on this peaceful shore for ever and ever, and Samsara's tumult is over there, seemingly so close, but as good as a million million miles away across the ocean. Will that do? Is that all?"

"That is all I want, that is all anyone could ever want," whispered Chiao, prostrating himself again and again. And adding, almost inaudibly, forehead on the ground, "The Holy One will, of course, honour without delay his gracious' promises to this simple monk."

"Instantly on waking, everything I have promised shall be yours, on these conditions. You must really want it, and you must let it in, open yourself to it, actually look at it and look out of it, instead of thinking about it and believing in it and reciting it. In actual fact, it's all yours anyway, unconditionally, whether you choose to let it in or not."

Next morning, Chiao recounted his dream to his young friend.

"It was a tremendous experience, while it lasted," he said very sadly. "What a pity it was only a dream, and not a word of it has come true. I suppose one can't expect a dream-Buddha's promises to hold good in a waking world, But they were so very definite, no ifs or buts about them at all. And he couldn't have been more glorious to look at, more beautiful."

"I gather the Holy One did mention," responded the novice, "that you must really want these immense boons, and then be humble enough to accept them just as they are given."

"Of course I really want them, and you should know how humble I am."

Tsung bowed repeatedly. "Then perhaps you already have them all, but just don't notice them," he said.

"What utter nonsense!" retorted Chiao, sharply, as he got ready to recite the Heart Sutra for the ten-thousand-and-first time.

22

THE
RESURRECTION

Don't imagine the resurrection is an illusion.
It is no illusion, it's the truth.
The resurrection is the revelation of what is,
the transformation of things,
a transition into newness.
Why not see yourself as already risen?
Treatise on the Resurrection (3rd century AD)

Basic to the Christian faith is the Apostles' Creed, which includes the words: "I believe in ... the resurrection of the body." Not only the resurrection of the spirit (please note) but of the flesh. Quintus Septimius Tertullian (c. 160–240), who was perhaps the greatest early exponent of the faith, couldn't be more explicit about this. The body that's raised from the dead, he insists, is none other than "this very flesh which is saturated with blood, supported by bones, interwoven with nerves and with veins." Such is the physique of the risen Christ, and of us all on the far side of the grave. And why should we believe this? *Because it's absurd!* It's certain because it's impossible. This is in all seriousness called Tertullian's Rule of Faith, which St. Augustine lines up with in due course.

For almost two thousand years countless believers, some of

them as brilliant intellectually as St Thomas Aquinas, others as luminous and God-centred as Ruysbroeck and St Catherine of Genoa, have recited and endorsed and believed in this patent absurdity, this impossibility, this *Ruling-out* of Faith!

Why this perennial nonsense that knows how nonsensical it is?

Now it seems to me that belief in "the rising of *Jesus Christ* from the dead on the third day", though a strain on one's credulity, is by no means impossible. After all, he was still physically intact though not functioning, all there for his contemporaries to see and to handle and to recognise. And nowadays, of course, there's a fast-growing number of patients who, having been diagnosed as clinically dead, nevertheless recover and came back to tell their story. I'm not suggesting that Jesus was one of these so-called NDE cases, but only that their stories about Death's door make his through-the-door story rather less implausible.

What *is* quite absurd is the belief that, come Judgement Day, the molecules that once constituted a cremated or drowned or long-buried body should, all-ears for the Last Trump, obediently rush together from far and wide and organise themselves into a living version of the deceased. Add to this wildest of fairy tales the problem that many or most of 'your' molecules belong to other resurrection bodies! I can foresee countless bitter disputes, and nearly all the risen bodies horribly deformed and emaciated due to shortage of material. As for the problems which cannibalism throws in, the imagination boggles.

Why (I repeat) this ancient and hallowed nonsense, not just believed in but insisted on by hordes of otherwise sensible people?

One answer, which I'm sure is valid so far as it goes, has been suggested by a number of writers. It amounts to this. We have a deep-seated instinct that there must be an after-life, and that to be real this after-life must be a bodily life, no matter what impossibilities that life may entail. A Heaven inhabited only by disembodied spirits – invisible, intangible, inaudible, odourless – would (we feel sure) be more like a Cosmic Gasometer or Weather Forecast than a Togetherness of loving persons.

The trouble with this attempt to account for the hold which

the dogma of bodily resurrection, in spite of all its absurdities, has had on Western man, is that it does nothing to get rid of those absurdities. On the contrary, it adds to them, by posing such questions as the following. Can it be that our true well-being, the very meaning of our life, is founded on a nonsense, on a bare-faced lie, on stark staring madness? Is that the sort of Universe we find ourselves marooned in? Has God, suffering from senile dementia, got things dreadfully muddled up? Or is He a trickster who has arranged that the truth about these life-and-death matters shall consist of untruths? And, instead of setting us free, shall shut us up in a mad-house?

Of course we may be driven to such desperate beliefs as a last resort, after we have tried what saner alternatives are on offer and found them to be either non-existent or else unworkable. Meanwhile let's admit the possibility (if not the probability) that the fault lies in ourselves, in our wilful blindness to the truth rather than the truth itself. That almost certainly it is we and not the gods who have gone crazy.

Well, there is a saner alternative.

The alternative I propose is that you and I should dare to *look and SEE what we ALREADY are, no matter what we think or are told we are.* And that we should go on to record as carefully as we can what we see.

I'll show you what I find myself to be, on the understanding that you look and see whether you too are like that when you sit or stand in front of a full-length mirror and draw the body you see in it, together with what you see of the body that's this side of the glass, making the drawing. No prizes are offered for artistic merit, but the Prize offered for veracity is priceless.

I'm in no position to speak for you, but when I'm in front of a full-length mirror, I see two bodies, two contrasting versions of what I call myself, as illustrated below.

Yes, what I get is two bodies, and I can't do with less. They go together.

The smaller one I christen *my pre-mortem body* because it has

179

yet to die. And the larger one I
christen *my post-mortem body*
because it has already died – by
beheading, which
is the most
summary
mode of
execution – and
come to life again.
To a life that
couldn't be more
self-evident and lively
and familiar. I have
to agree wholeheartedly with

Tertullian's description of my resurrection body as "this flesh
which is saturated with blood, supported by bones, interwoven
with nerves and with veins." Where we disagree is that while he
believed in it because it was an absurdity that lies in the future, I
believe in it because it's an obviousness that lies in the present.

Tertullian's orthodox version of the resurrection of the body
has to be absurd because it finds no differences between my post-
mortem body and my pre-mortem body. Whereas in fact those
differences are many and profound and striking. Some of them
appear in our drawing, the chief of which is the absence in the
smaller body of a timeless centre, and its presence in the larger
one. Just now I want to stress and revel in the fact that the life I'm
actually living, willy-nilly and here and now, is a *risen* life, the life
of this post-mortem resurrection body, and by no means the life of
that pre-mortem pre-resurrection body. It's this decapitated torso
that itches, not that capitated torso. I believe this because it's
obvious.

Amazingly it's a life we deny we are living, just don't want to
know about. Think of all those hundreds and hundreds of
fascinating portraits on show in the National Portrait Gallery in
London – Winston Churchill and Virginia Woolf and G.K.Chesterton
and all the rest of them. Was a single one of them *that way round,
looking in that direction*? Were any of them *in that thing, looking*

at the world out of those two eyes? Did those capitated bodies ever *itch*? Did even the most saintly of them all contain *an imperishable Core*?

The answer, of course, is a resounding No. The *real* Winston, the *real* Virginia, the *real* G.K., together with all the others, sported a very different, decapitated, other-way-round, itching *resurrection* body, at least one metre distant from that painting or photo or mirror-image. (How many of them realised that huge difference, and consciously lived the resurrection life, is of course quite another matter.)

I'm not saying, mind you, that I've got this resurrection life all neatly buttoned up and accounted for and comprehended. Quite the contrary. Obvious doesn't mean obedient or obliging, or understood, or unmysterious. In fact, I can't think of any state of affairs more open-ended, more adventurous and truly mind-boggling than this risen life. And – praise the Lord! – this built-in ambiguity happens to be just what the doctor ordered, exactly what I want of this new life. Namely, that it shall magisterially combine the changeless Core with its changing instruments, certainty and security and rest with their opposites, profound knowledge with open-mouthed ignorance, I've got it all cut and dried with I'm flabbergasted.

But please don't *believe* a word of all this. Try it out. Repeatedly photograph, or preferably draw, those juxtaposed bodies of yours, decide which you are living in and out of right now, and adjust your sights and your life as needed.

Let's now try to make sense of another aspect of the 'Tertullian absurdity'.

Our resurrection life (we are told) is spent in Heaven, way up there in the realm of the stars and other heavenly bodies. In fact this is an age-old tradition common to most cultures. You could say that not only do we have an instinct that there is a resurrection life which is a bodily life, but also that it's *lived in the sky*. Of course this doesn't mean that the instinct is therefore true or well-founded, but it certainly does mean that we need to look and see what truth there is in it.

At first glance the location seems unlikely. The climate of the heavens is, to put it mildly, unsuitable for human consumption. We would all die of pneumonia long before we got there.

To do justice to this question we must take account of the full range of cosmic levels above and below the human level, the great hierarchy of wholes and parts to which man belongs. And when – pulling ourselves together – you and I do so, we find we have not just two but three bodies on our hands. In order of decreasing abstractness and increasing concreteness and completeness, they are:

(1) My Pre-mortem Body, (2) my Post-mortem Resurrection Body, and (3) my Total or Cosmic Body. Roughly, this is the form these three bodies take:

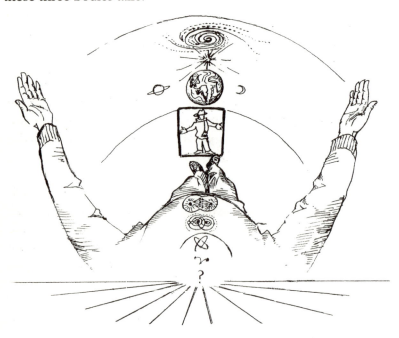

This sketch of Body (3) indicates what Bodies (1) and (2) *need, what they must have in order to be what they are.* To find out what this is I ask myself: What am I without my fellow humans and the things they get up to, without Earth's air and soil and water and flora and fauna, without the Sun's light and energy, without the Cosmos itself? Again, I ask myself: What am I without the cells I consist of and that do all I do, and what are they without the molecules they consist of, and what are they without the atoms they consist of, and so on down into the abyss? And the answer to this most searching and comprehensive of questions is: Without them all I'm less than a shadow, an abstraction, a dream. Truly, truly this magnificent hierarchy of wholes and parts is *indivisible*, and to be this special Douglasy thing in it I have to embrace and include all those other special things as well, along with the Nothing or Zero at our Common Source and Centre.

It follows that (as indicated in the illustration above) I, the resurrected one, am already in Heaven and *couldn't live anywhere else*. And if people tell me that the stars are light-years distant, I tell them that the stars I see are right here and now, and anyway the 'distance' between me and them reads as a point, as no distance at all when seen end-on, which is the way I do see it.

A last-minute but serious objection occurs to me here. When I make for my Home-base or Centre of Gravity or Headquarters in this gigantic Body of mine, I find myself sinking to the bottom of the picture beneath the quarks instead of rising to the top of it above the stars. Sinking to the place that's surely more like Hades (or should I say Hell?) than Heaven.

So what do I do?

I point to this abysmal Centre-point that I'm looking out of, and I find myself to be a Nothing that's consciously exploding in all directions, instantaneously. Molecular bombs containing TNT are powerful and dirty, atomic bombs are more powerful and dirtier, nuclear bombs are still more powerful and still dirtier. But this explosion of the Zero Bomb right here and now is infinitely powerful and perfectly clean, and it is the transformation of Nothing into Everything. It is also none other than the Great Resurrection from the Dead into Life as this Glorious All-level Body and World without end, Amen.

I'm quite sure of this Resurrection because, unlike dear old Tertullian (who had all the right instincts for all the wrong reasons), I find that, instead of being future and absurd it's present and obvious, thank God!

And that's it!

23

HE WHO CREATED ME RESTED IN MY TENT[1]

"My dear friend," He said to me, "what have you got to lose by doing Me the favour of letting Me be God in you?"[2]

"No guest could be more welcome, dear Lord," I reply, "and no host more awe-struck and overcome with gratitude. You are my heart's desire – as You well know."

"Yes, I know. But I'd like to hear how things stand between us, what is the present state of our union as you see it. Something along the lines of the American President's annual State of the Union Address, perhaps."

"Well. Lord, I have to confess to all sorts of bad impulses and idle imaginings. I'm your property absolutely, I house my Lord, but alas I'm semi-detached, so to say."

"These are just the sort of problems to bring you to Me. But please don't change the subject. We aren't talking about the state of your mind but the state of our union."

"I can't think where to begin ..."

"What about the Eye that really is Wide Open? How goes it?"

"Wonderfully well, dear Lord! Nothing could be simpler or more natural – yet more astonishing – than looking out of this colossal Eye."

"Our Eye!"

"Thank You, Lord. Than looking out of our Eye, whose immensity is such that it sees itself off in all directions, and whose clarity is such that it clears itself of all traces of itself, of everything. In fact, I can't think what it was like to imagine I was peering at Your world through a pair of tiny peep-holes in a kind of Hallowe'en pumpkin. What a gift Your wider-than-worldwide Eye is, how generously given, how blazingly obvious!"

"And quite a lot comes with it. Pay attention to your Eye, and I'll see that you get the rest of Me thrown in for good measure. How *could* I present you with such a vital part of Myself and withhold the rest? I come Whole, or not at all. And I come easy, as easy as winking. A little curiosity and wonder, a little practice that isn't practice but enjoyment, and you have not only caught the habit of seeing with Me but as Me!"

"And they say You play hard-to-get!"

"Along with My Eye comes My Hand."

"Why yes, Lord, they go together naturally. Here's something quite wonderful! These hands are mine inasmuch as they do my human work, and these arms are mine inasmuch as they embrace my human love. Yet these very same hands are Yours inasmuch as they do Your divine work."

"What other sort do I have? And it's as you, dear one, that I embrace the one you love. Don't imagine that you can become Me without Me becoming you. We need each other. Man can't become God without God returning the compliment."

"What an impossible miracle these commonplace limbs really are! The things they get up to! Yet again, how natural, how readily put forth, how childlike! Here's a drawing, by a child of eight, of herself vis-à-vis a friend."

Note the cut-off arms put forth by her Spaciousness, not by her shoulders and trunk like the arms of her friend. I wonder: how could what comes so naturally and effortlessly at eight be unnatural at eighteen, or virtually impossible at eighty?"

"Or be withheld from anyone who's mildly interested, at any time? The trouble with you humans is that you slip so easily from the rock-solid ground of percepts into a morass of concepts. Let's be practical. Give Me a concrete instance of the two modes of functioning of these hands and arms of ours, of the spectacular contrast between these modes."

"I'm trying, Lord, to think of a telling instance. Perhaps in the stillness of a meditation hall or zendo I would come up with a good one."

"What about your car, as a more convenient and regular and certainly more comfortable sort of zendo? Not as a rule noted for its stillness, but …"

"Why of course, dear Lord! Of course! These very human hands of mine that put on my socks and wash dishes and tap at keyboards do very different things when they handle the steering wheel of my car. Divine things, Lord, Your things! – provided I go by what You show me instead of what people tell me. Then, instead of driving me to Paris, these hands drive Paris to me. At my rear, instead of driving me away from Calais, they drive Calais away from me. Sideways, instead of driving me past still countryside at 70 mph, they drive the countryside past me at many speeds. Yes! These very same hands that peel potatoes in my kitchen peel Your Universe, layer by layer, in my Renault Clio! And all the while I stay put in Your Stillness, the Stillness that moves all things!"

"Was it so very difficult to break the tiring and dangerous habit of driving without due care and attention? To turn your Clio into your Zendo, in which Meditation = Attention = Astonishment = Union-with-Me?"

"Not that difficult, dear Lord. For a long time now I've found it impossible to halt the scenery, hijacking as much of its horse-power as I can to fuel my Clio. All thanks to my Divine Chauffeur!"

"Well, I'm doing My level best to make our union as interesting, as vivid and as inescapable, as intimate and as easy, as funny-peculiar and as funny-ha!-ha! as possible. Really I don't see what more I could do, short of whisking you and Me into a divine-human mulligatawny that would drown us both. No, the price of the never-ending joy of our coming together is our never-ending and freely-chosen separateness.'

"Grudgingly, Lord, I pay up. All the same, I insist that as What these hands and arms are visibly sticking out of – as this Boundless and Timeless Clarity at Centre – You and I and all creatures are absolutely and forever One and the Same, the Same, the Same."

"Exactly so, dear one. A pair of Nothings – any number of Nothings – can't help rushing together instantly to become One Nothing. Nor can this One Nothing help exploding instantly into Everything. But let's look at some of its down-to-earth, everyday consequences. What would you say they are?"

"Well, this Nothing – this Boundless Clarity – for sure transforms personal relationships. Living from this Nothing, I'm left with nothing to confront anyone with. How can I avoid vanishing in favour of her or him or it? The truth is that in You, Lord, and as You, I give my life, my very being, for that one. This act of total self-abandonment, so impossible for me as me, becomes possible and even natural for me as You. As united to You whose generosity goes to such lengths that You hand over Your divine perfections to me. To me, and You know how desperately I need them! He in whom God dwells has a good lodger, no matter how lousy the lodgings."

"So far, so good. The state of our union as you see it – and indeed as I see it – seems satisfactory, to say the least. There's plenty for us to share and be amused at and very happy about, and little or nothing that's really difficult for you to put into practice day by day."

"And more than enough to keep me overwhelmed with gratitude. But …"

"Some real difficulties remain?"

"I'm afraid so, Lord. Let me try to explain. He who created me rests in my tent. There were and there are and there must be two of us – Creator and created – and where there's two there's terror. And heartache. My problem is that I can't do with less than all of You. Ironically, dear One, though I need You arrayed in all Your splendour, in all Your majesty and mystery as the Origin of Yourself and me and all the rest, it's this very splendour that holds us far apart. Eff the ineffable, and what's left? The very attributes I insist on Your having ensure I don't get You!"

"You mean to tell Me that, far beyond and above all that we share, is My unshareable knack of Self-origination and World-origination?"

"Precisely, Lord."

"Then here's a surprise for you. I'm able and willing and eager to share with you that very special expertise. The fact is that I'm doing so already, and you take no notice."

"My dearest Love, I can't imagine ... "

"Of course you can't. Don't try. I guess it's My turn to do some explaining. You tell Me that you are utterly amazed that there's anything at all. You add that you are bowled over with wonder and admiration at My "impossible" stunt of popping up, with no help and for no reason, from the long, dark night of cosmic Oblivion. Well, listen to Me! Don't kid yourself that you as you are capable of this Astonishment to end all astonishment. It's Mine alone. And yours alone because I am you."

"Why of course, Lord! How could this all-too-human human, as such, begin to get around to this divine Wonder? – if I may call it that. No. I've no problem with Your primary Self-creation. It's Your secondary and cosmic creativity, the sort that really does belong to You alone, that parts us."

"What nonsense you talk! I can no more give you my Eye minus its knack of creating and destroying and re-creating things than you can give Me your hand minus it knack of feeling the shape and texture of things. Come on, don't be so silly!"

"O my Lord!"

"For Heaven's sake go by what you see, by what I'm showing you with all My might. Shut Eye, shut down the world. Open Eye, open it up again."

"*Why of course, Lord, a million times of course!!!* Forgive my abysmal obtuseness! It's the things You make specially plain that I make specially obscure, make a special muck of. Make impossible, without Your help."

"It's a funny way you have of teasing Me, I suppose. A sort of love-play."

"Talking of love-play, dear One, there's a kind that's tremendously important for me, *profoundly* important. "Praise to the Holiest in the height," sang John Henry Newman, "And in the depth be praise." Our shared Eye, Lord, with its shared powers, is the most exalted and (at long, long last) the most obvious proof and demonstration and bodying forth of our indissoluble union. But it's in the depth that I get the feel of our union so strongly ..."

"Yes I know. But tell Me."

"For many years now I've been in the habit of silently repeating to myself, from time to time, my own secret mantra *"To be saved is to be Him"*, while breathing out very deeply indeed. My whole body down to my toenails seems to be expiring, breathing me out and You in. The strong sensation of leaning back and collapsing into Your Immensity, of merging with You utterly, brings with it the profoundest physical relaxation I know. As I say, it's as if, breathing out thus deeply, *I* breathe *You* in; and, breathing in again, *You* breathe *me* in. It's very much as if, having just saved me from drowning in the Sea of Death, You were giving me the Kiss of Life."

"What a mutual joy that is! And I can't think of a happier or truer note on which to end today's conversation about the state of our union."

HE WHO CREATED ME RESTED IN MY TENT AND ALL NIGHT THERE WAS THE SOUND OF ONE BREATHING

Note 1
This is a quotation from Eckhart (Walshe, Eckhart: *Sermons and Treatises*, Watkins and Element Books II p.13.) who got it from *Ecclesiasticus*.

Note 2
Some years ago I recorded this passage, attributing it to Eckhart. But I can't find it in Walshe's 3-volume English translation of Eckhart (op. cit.), or in Miss Evans' 2-volume translation (also Watkins) on which Walshe drew. In fact, it's almost certainly not Eckhart's at all. I've no idea who I got it from – other than the One who's addressing me in the dialogue that follows. In any case my most shocking inefficiency as a student of mystical texts subserves His gracious plan to put to me, right now and directly, His intention to "rest in my tent".

24

THAT IS THE ANSWER

Why is TO BE *and* NOT TO BE the answer? The answer to the terrifying and endless questions that life poses?

In the course of our free-ranging enquiry we have touched on the following reasons.

1. It respects the basic facts as given, requires me to understand and live in the light of what's evidently so. Looking out, I see that I am; looking in, I see that I am not.

2. I need both. I need Being, and release from Being. Not-Being overcomes the pain of Being, of existence, while Being overcomes the pain of Not-Being, of extinction. Together, they get on with the job. It's rather like having your cake and eating it, or making the best of both worlds. A good thing to do – if you can.

3. Being and Non-Being don't stay opposed and at odds. They fit, are inseparable halves of the Whole. They come together nicely in all the changing circumstances of my life – provided I let them do so. And their union happens to be what my problems need to set them right.

4. Here's an example. I find in myself two powerful but seemingly incompatible urges. I want to win, to come out on top, to be very special and indeed unique. And I want to be relieved of all

that bother, free as the wind, in the clear, exempt. Now instead of perversely inciting these two contrary forces to pull me apart, I let them do their real job of pulling me together.

5. And here's another example. Love is the best gift that life has to offer, and one of the most problem-ridden. And the perfect union of Being and Non-Being is at once the ground and the dynamic of love. So that to love is to vanish in favour of the loved one. Visibly to disappear, to be out of the way. First the vision: the feeling will follow as and when it should.

So over to you!

None of this is for believing, all is for testing in daily life. I have told you what it's like *where* I am. Is it like this *where* you are?